MOTHERING

WITHOUT

A COMPASS

Also by Becky Thompson

A Hunger So Wide and So Deep: A Multiracial View of Women's Eating Problems

Beyond a Dream Deferred: Multicultural Education and the Politics of Excellence (with Sangeeta Tyagi)

Names We Call Home: Autobiography on Racial Identity (with Sangeeta Tyagi)

Becky Thompson

MOTHERING

White Mother's Love

WITHOUT

Black Son's Courage

A COMPASS

University of Minnesota Press
Minneapolis • London

Published by the University of Minnesota Press
111 Third Avenue South, Suite 290
Minneapolis, MN 55401-2520
http://www.upress.umn.edu

Library of Congress Cataloging-in-Publication Data

Thompson, Becky W.
    Mothering without a compass : white mother's love, Black son's
courage / Becky Thompson.
        p.   cm.
    Includes bibliographical references.
    ISBN 0-8166-3635-4 (alk. paper) — ISBN 0-8166-3636-2 (pbk. : alk.
paper)
        1. Lesbian mothers — United States — Family relationships.   2. White
women — United States — Family relationships.   3. Afro-American young
men — Family relationships.   4. Children of gay parents — United
States — Family relationships.   5. Mother and son — United States.
I. Title.
HQ75.53 .T48   2000
306.874'3 — dc21   00-009339

Printed in the United States of America on acid-free paper

The University of Minnesota is an equal-opportunity educator and
employer.

11 10 09 08 07 06 05 04 03 02 01 00   10 9 8 7 6 5 4 3 2 1

To
Katie Cannon,
Sheila Hart,
and the young ones
at the center of my heart.

Contents

Put my head in her hands,

our two heads together

I HAD KNOWN FOR MANY YEARS that I was going to be a mother. In fact, I had had a recurring feeling since early adulthood that a child would simply arrive on my doorstep. My intuition was that I wouldn't even have to go and fill out papers. A child would simply show up at my house. So, I wasn't very surprised when Adrian—the younger brother of Andrea, a marvelous, twenty-one-year-old woman who had become my goddaughter a few years earlier—arrived for a two-week summer vacation in August 1997 and then announced a week later that he was staying for good.

When Adrian's mother called a few days later to ask if I would continue to care for him, I was afraid my excitement might make me rush to control a conversation that was really hers to initiate. My mind raced, wondering what I would need to know as a white lesbian to raise an African American boy in a country that so complicates that arrangement. My heart beat hard, but I hadn't been surprised that Adrian's mother had called. I do remember feeling flushed after we hung up, after I told her I would be honored to care for him, and that I would love him as much as any human being could. And I remember feeling grateful that Andrea was just downstairs, so I could tell her the news in person, put my head in her hands, put our two heads together, and be quiet for the moment while I felt my life turning in a new direction, forever changed.

Since then, I have often felt like a skittery deer, darting from store to store in search of a book, a poem, an essay, even a title that could give words to what this experience is doing to me, what this experience is requiring of me. I have been reading as if my life depended on it, wanting so much to know how people raising adopted children talk with them about betrayal, abandonment, and loneliness. I want so much to read writing by white and Black women who are raising Black sons. I want to have, already on my bookshelves, easily reached, writing about the vulnerability, joy, terror, and deep loneliness I feel as I am learning to mother. I search through store after store, in hopes of finding a book that will tell this story, only to realize that no *one* book will do. This is a story of discontinuity, not found in any one place, best reckoned with if I accept fragmentation as an inevitable part of my past, his past, and our present together.

By night, and in fifteen-minute snatches between work and picking Adrian up from school, I search for books. By day, I search people's eyes, wondering if they will be up to the task of hearing me out — about mundane issues that I am encountering for the first time, but that most mothers of nine-year-olds have long since figured out. I scroll down in my brain, in my telephone book, wondering which friend I can call, who I can talk with without having to explain much.

I have never felt so compartmentalized in all my life. One conversation with this person. Another conversation with that person. No full conversation with any one person. An old colleague, an African American woman who is an antiracist educator, knows about the scapegoating Adrian is facing at school and how that has everything to do with his being African American and a new student. Another friend, an Indian mother of two young boys, knows about the deep exhaustion I feel as a new mother, a new mother of a nine-year-old who has energy all day and much to spare late into the night. Andrea knows so much about Adrian's past, and I find myself craving any details she can give me about where Adrian has lived, what he is used to eating, how he has dealt with anger in the past, and what will comfort him when he is tired. But Andrea wants to say little, as he reminds her of where she was during a period in her life that she, understandably, wants to distance herself from, along with so much she has seen and they have seen together.

In moments when I am overwhelmed, I feel like I am cut up in a thousand pieces—running around trying to find advice about race, about adoption, about class, about culture, about mothering, from a community of people already fragmented by these issues. In calmer moments, I understand that the fragmentation is as much about me as about anyone else—it is about my own inability with words, my own confusion, my own difficulties with saying the whole story, even if there were a single person who could hear it all. With that realization, I see that I am running around looking for myself.

The desperate desire I have to write, to read, to think, comes from wanting to make sense of a story that has already been cut into pieces. How do you splice film that comes from so many cameras—from Polaroids, from

35-millimeters, from disposable point-and-shoots? How do you splice together film based on footage that has not been shot — about conversations that the politics of race and mothering have made difficult, if not impossible, to have?

In moments of panic, I feel like I need to create a village from scratch. There are whole categories of people I need to know now in a way I didn't before. African American mothers of Black children. White mothers of Black children. Writing mothers of small children. White lesbians with children of color. Black children who play with action figures and Beanie Babies. White children who already have African American playmates — so that Adrian won't be their first.

At other times, I realize, gratefully, that most of the village now surrounding Adrian seems to have been miraculously awaiting his arrival. Longtime friends who self-named themselves his uncles and aunts. A Jewish friend and writer, Jo, who raised her now-grown daughter within a multiracial community, so that seeing African American and Latina women around her house when she was growing up was, itself, unremarkable. A white woman student of mine, Kerry, who emancipated herself from her abusive family when she was only thirteen, and her Nigerian fiancé, Kayode, who immediately referred to themselves as Adrian's aunt and uncle. Both take Adrian out on adventures regularly. Recently made friends who knew to bring Adrian a fancy warm coat for his first winter in Boston. A close friend who knew that getting Adrian into a private school was one thing that I, with much help from activist connections, could do. Paying for it I couldn't do, without her help, which she provided immediately. In calmer moments I understand that three months into it, a community has already created itself. Not enough. Not complete. But remarkable nevertheless.

Of course, I didn't have a clue at first about what I'd need to begin to mother Adrian. I didn't know that mothering him would force me, enable me, to become close to a whole community of people I might never have met otherwise. I didn't have one moment to reflect, to ask myself how to learn what I was going to need to know. The first few weeks with Adrian in my life were frantic. Yes, I made time to play basketball together; to introduce him to J. P. Licks, a neighborhood ice-cream store that has long been a hallmark of this intentionally multiracial, mixed-class community in Boston where I live; to take him to the pond with my three dogs (who are quickly becoming his three dogs, too). I did find time to begin introducing him around.

What I most remember, though, about the first few weeks was my utter panic about how to get Adrian into a racially diverse private school—no small task given that school was starting in ten days. In Boston, the progressive private schools have long, long waiting lists of parents who know that private grammar schools and high schools are the feeder schools to private colleges. I remember feeling weary at the thought of having to call people I had never met, of having to explain, from the beginning, in compelling and brief terms, why I was calling at the last minute, why it was essential for them to make a space for Adrian in their school.

When I was a postdoctoral fellow in African American studies several years ago, I was struck by a discussion I heard following a talk by Cornel West. A student asked

Professor West whether he thought it was problematic for white parents to send their children to private schools. In effect the student was asking whether buying an education was a 1990s version of upholding the 1896 *Plessy vs. Ferguson* "separate and unequal" Supreme Court ruling. I expected Cornel West to say that people shouldn't give up on public schools, that integration was crucial, and that learning side-by-side across race and class was necessary to break open racial locks. But he didn't say that. Instead he said that he understood why white families might send their children to private schools. He said that it wasn't fair to compromise individual children's education as long as their education might well suffer because of underfunding and poor resources.

I remember being shocked by his answer because I had been raised to believe that white people, especially, should not abandon public schools. To do so was to cash in on a class and race privilege not available to everyone. Plus, I had been raised to believe that private education would somehow stunt children's growth. If they were isolated by race and class in childhood, they would be destined to repeat that narrow mind-set as adults. And yet I was also compelled by Cornel West's answer — by his honesty and his willingness to confront a party line I had barely questioned.

While I stored his position away in my head, I continued to speak out in support of public schools, and of the activism necessary to keep them alive, right up to the day that Andrea, Adrian, and I arrived at a local "exam" high school in Boston to talk about the school's crew program. A 1984 Olympic-champion-turned-extraordinary-crew-coach had asked Andrea and me to speak as a "mother-

daughter" team about the thrills of crew for young women.
I had originally met Andrea, the captain of a crew team at
a private university in Connecticut, when I was teaching
at the school and rowing with a masters women's crew
team. The fact that crew had initially brought us together
only increased our excitement about the sport, individu-
ally and as intergenerational devotees.

Andrea, Adrian, and I arrived at the public high school
with Adrian's Legos in tow, which we hoped would occupy
him for two hours of presentations by school administrators before the athletic department (including us) would
get a chance to speak. The Legos did work, for a while,
until Adrian picked up on Andrea's and my anxiety-turned-
to-rage about what we saw. At this school, which, as an
"exam" school, is supposed to be one of the best in the
Boston public school system, one administrator after
another lectured the parents—about how their children
were ill prepared, about how there would be repercus-
sions if the parents couldn't "control their children," about
how lucky the parents should feel that their children had
been accepted at a school that looked frighteningly like a
prison. The lectures had no substance. The administrators
said nothing about a goal of educating African American,
Caribbean, Latino/a, and Asian American youth to be
leaders for the twenty-first century. They did not mention
the skills, initiative, and family support that helped get
these children to an exam school. And they were silent
about how and why the school might fight for its share
of the resources and then some.

Andrea, who had been shuttled from school to school
to school when growing up but who had landed at a private school her last two years of high school, got more

and more antsy as the administrators railed on. And we both began to feel rage. Rage at the condescension aimed at the parents, many of whom had no doubt arranged for time off from work that morning to accompany their children to this nonevent. Rage at the realities of racism and classism that for two centuries have blocked what would be a simple and elegant step toward abolishing educational apartheid in this country: assign the exact same amount of money per child, per head, regardless of differences in property taxes and local, state, or regional commitments to education.

As the speakers droned on and on, I also got madder and madder at myself, for my naïveté, for the liberal line on education that I had both accepted for myself and supported in my teaching—a position that had little grounding in what I was seeing and feeling that day. Andrea whispered to me that I had to do whatever I needed to be sure that Adrian did not have to "go to a school like this." And I saw my long-carried belief that I would work with other parents to make the public school what it needed to be evaporate. I wouldn't do that. I couldn't do that. How do you make a building that looks like a prison not look like one? How do you change a school—in time for your own child—that the whole tax structure and history of racism in Boston have underfunded for years?

I became part of white flight in that moment—white flight with an African American child—and I understood Cornel West's position. I didn't yet have a clue about how I could come up with the money I would need to pay for a private education. Childless person I had been, I had almost no knowledge of which private schools to seek out, how to apply, or whom to call. The horrendous experience

Adrian had had at the neighborhood camp that summer —
being called a "sissy," a "faggot," and "not Black enough,"
being told to kneel on the floor with his hands up on a
table edge with thirty other children for half an hour because they were "bad" — let me know that I had to do my
homework fast.

Andrea and I went to a secondhand store in Brookline
(since the best secondhand stores are where rich people
live), where we bought him a barely used J. Crew oxford-
cloth shirt that I then washed and ironed four times, for
four interviews at private schools in the area. Adrian, gre-
garious and openhearted child that he is, smiled and talked
and answered the many questions asked of him. He took
several standardized tests, as well as those designed by
each school. After the second interview, he said he couldn't
possibly do one more. He slept all the way in the car — a
forty-five-minute drive — to the third interview, even though
he had just slept a full night through. I remember trying
to drive quietly (as if that is possible in Boston, the car-
honking capital of the country), hoping that sleep would
give him whatever strength he needed to go on a tour of
yet another school, meet another set of teachers, and take
another diagnostic test.

I became part of white flight as I began calling every
educator and activist I knew — African American, Latino,
and white — in hopes that they might know someone,
somewhere, who might know someone on an admissions
committee someplace, who might be willing to meet Adrian
and me, ten days before school started, to interview for a
place in a school that I knew full well had been filled at
least a year before. In those moments, I understood I was
working a class privilege by using contacts I had through

the private college where I taught, to call administrators in other private schools, who themselves, or their children, had attended private schools. I knew that I was trying to find a "legacy" way into a private school through a process of nonbiological associations. No surprise that the people who found me a "way in" were mostly people of color. In fact, I got the most help from a Latino dean of a college that specializes in education—a man whose children attend a private school and who is a member of the board of trustees at a prep school in the area. He made calls that got Adrian an interview with the dean of admissions at three private schools, all of whom accepted Adrian within a few days of our applications, five days before the start of the school year.

Witness to the telling

I WAS, OF COURSE, relieved to see that schools were making a way for Adrian so few days before school was going to start. And I was relieved when a progressive school founded on principles of nonviolence not only accepted him, but offered a financial aid package that I could live with for a year — if I lived paycheck to paycheck and was able to let down my I-am-afraid-to-ask-for-help guard and accept the generous monthly help from Hannah, a friend who had been family to me for over a decade and with whom I had recently become lovers. Of the four schools Adrian and I visited, Silver Street School was my top choice because three African American women educators I know had been satisfied overall that they had sent their children there. And, I had long respected the school's commitment to justice work.

It helped, too, when Andrea, Adrian, and I arrived at the interview and were greeted by Jewel McLeod, an African American woman who is the director of admissions. While she asked questions to make sense of how Adrian came to be with me in Boston, she also seemed to understand how class related to our situation. When Andrea and Adrian left the room briefly and I quietly said to Jewel that I had put myself through school and now had school loans until way past the year 2000, Jewel looked at me directly, and, with knowing and reassuring eyes, said so did she. I explained that although I was now supporting Andrea and Adrian, I did not want Adrian's education to be compromised by lack of funds. Jewel understood that Adrian needed a safe school (where there were no knives or guns), a small school, and a lively school, where there would be other brown faces in the halls, in the classrooms, and on the playground. Jewel understood that Adrian needed a school where there was a commitment to class and race diversity — not just because it was the right thing to do politically, but because it made for academic excellence in the classroom.

When Jewel asked Adrian what he knew about cities in the United States, he told her that he had learned in the Catholic school he attended last year that Detroit was a wealthy city because so many cars were made there. Jewel said that was true. She added that at Silver Street School, they might also talk about what happened to the workers when the American car companies began moving their plants to other countries and how that affected the school system in that city. I loved watching her infuse a social studies curriculum with a race and class analysis. And I could have kissed Jewel when she told Adrian that he could take home the essay he needed to write — that she was flexible enough to see that doing it at home was the only way an essay would get written that day.

Adrian had dutifully answered questions for the first fifteen minutes of the interview, but then began to slump lower and lower in his chair, saying that he was too tired to talk anymore. I was thankful that I was able to just look into Jewel's eyes and see that she understood, without my needing to explain, that Adrian would be able to hold his own in a fourth-grade class. With me, however, he was going to need to be a toddler sometimes, too. And at this moment, the toddler needed a nap. That was the first time I saw Adrian needing to be two ages at once — the nine-year-old who could sit at a school computer and find his way onto the Internet unassisted, and the two-year-old who could crawl into my lap, burrow between my breasts, and say he needed to sleep immediately.

At Silver Street School, what I cared about most was the critical mass of children of color and African American faculty and administrators who were in key positions. I was impressed that they had an up-and-running group for families of color and a well-organized antiracism committee, which included members of the board of trustees. My body relaxed when I saw the bulletin board in the school entryway announcing the fall meetings for the Gay and Lesbian Alliance. And I loved the vibrant mosaic of children running, smiling, and thinking that wrapped around the outside walls of the building. When we toured the building, I noticed all of the new construction, thinking that it would be good for Adrian to be at a spanking new school. I also remember thinking that all that building must have cost millions of dollars and that other markers of class I had yet to discover would be complicated for Adrian and me.

In the car after the interview, class was the first thing Andrea talked about — that it was an upper-middle-class school — a much better place for Adrian than a Boston public school, but still a school with children whose lives would be very different from Adrian's. Andrea also said the school felt a bit "precious" to her, a label that I have spent the first year feeling, seeing, and trying to make sense of.

Initially, a big draw for me was Silver Street's emphasis on teaching pacifism, peace, and conflict resolution. That mattered to me especially because Adrian had been physically and emotionally abused since he was very young. I wanted a place where adults would help young people deal with conflicts without physical violence and where adults might see children's whole selves. What I didn't know yet was how the scapegoating Adrian would face in the fall and spring would uncover the lie in the adage, "Sticks and stones may break my bones, but words will never hurt me."

Early in the fall, one of the teachers—a young white lesbian who had been teaching at Silver Street School for a few years—spoke to me on a Monday morning about a concern Adrian had shared with her the preceding Friday. He had told her that I had been punishing him by making him sit for half an hour at a time in a kneeling position while his hands had to be held high on a table. Having never done that, I was shocked and left the school visibly shaken. I spent the day reeling—dumbfounded that the teacher had accepted the story as a real possibility, confused by what the story meant, and overwhelmed by how to handle it at school.

By the time I arrived to pick Adrian up that afternoon, the story had unraveled. The African American counselor at the school (who had been meeting with me regularly) had met with Adrian and, unlike the teacher, had not believed him. He, probably with Adrian's help, had come to see that Adrian was speaking of a punishment that had been inflicted on him at a camp he had attended the preceding summer—a punishment Adrian had not told me about at the time. By afternoon, the teacher had apologized to me and the counselor had told Adrian that neither being punished that way, nor lying about me was okay. Adrian had also explained to me and the teacher that the punishment had happened at camp.

While Adrian's story stunned me at first, within days I began to uncover its meaning—that Adrian was testing the waters. If he called out "abuse," could he get noticed? Especially if it was abuse done by a parent? He had gotten noticed. Big time. Within six hours of his story, he had involved me, the two teachers, the school counselor, and the head of the lower school. I think he was testing all of us. That we would listen to him. That we would care. That we would take him seriously.

This experience may have been the precursor to his ability to write the teachers notes about kids picking on him. These notes, in concert with what the teachers observed, ultimately led them to tell me (in what turned out to be one of many teacher-parent meetings during the year) that Adrian was being scapegoated by a group of fourth- and fifth-grade white boys. The teachers thought it had to do with a combination of Adrian's being a new kid, a sensitive kid, and a Black kid. The teachers had witnessed times when the boys spoke in loud voices to the other children on the playground, but then yelled at Adrian. The children were pushing him around, while not doing the same to others. The teachers had observed that Adrian was mostly trying to keep to his own, clearly not knowing who could be safely trusted among his peers.

I was grateful that the teachers used the word "scapegoating" and that they attributed it to race (although by using the word "race," rather than "racism," they were identifying a description, a category, while leaving power out of the equation). By talking about the incidents in racialized terms, however, we could skip over basic discussions about how it matters that Adrian was one of only two African American boys in the class and the darker of the two. We could then be strategic together about what to do. I appreciated that the teachers said they were going to call the fifth-grade boys together and ask them to provide some leadership for the fourth-grade boys, and that they would talk with the fourth-grade boys as a group, telling them their treatment had to stop.

While I think the teachers' actions helped to stop some of the most blatant nastiness, what had the most impact on Adrian came from the African American after-school teacher, whom Adrian clearly adores. After meeting Christopher during his first week at school, Adrian put him on the top of the list of people to invite to our October "Welcome Adrian to the Family and Community" ritual. Christopher—with his dreadlocks and totally handsome self—arrived with a fertility necklace he had made for Adrian that matched the one he wore everyday. At the party, he put it on Adrian and then touched their necklaces together—letting Adrian know that they were spiritually bonded. When Adrian decided to say something to the gorgeous array of people who had come to celebrate his arrival, he, in an amazingly self-assured way, thanked the people from Silver Street School for coming, especially his after-school teacher, Christopher. The whole crowd applauded when he said that.

One afternoon later that fall, Christopher pulled Adrian and me aside and said, directly into Adrian's eyes, "You are one of the sweetest boys I have ever met, as sweet to people as I was when I was a kid. My heart goes out to you, because kids will take advantage of you and sometimes you will have to stand up for yourself. Hold your own, Adrian. Don't give in too easily. A lot of times you are right."

Watching his face as Christopher spoke, I saw Adrian listening more carefully than ever before. His face showed sheer thankfulness. Absolute respect. Definite bonding. And a clear message to me, that one of my tasks would be to help him take charge of his own space. The violence done to him had not yet made him try to fight back physically. His tendency was to withdraw and somehow make the violence "his fault." So far, he had responded to violence by withdrawing rather than by lashing out. In the moment when Christopher looked deeply at Adrian and spoke from his own childhood experience and adult wisdom, I felt in my bones that there could be no substitute for gentle, wise Black men in Adrian's life. Silver Street School had brought us one, although, at the time, there were only two African American men on staff, both part time.

Since the fall, the incidents of violence have continued. This past week, I asked the teachers to intervene again after Adrian told me that one of the fourth-grade white boys had hit him repeatedly—a boy who, earlier in the year, Adrian had said was someone he liked. Adrian had never fought back. The teachers spoke with the boy and he apologized. When I picked Adrian up at the end of school that day, he told me I had a way of getting things done without "making a big deal of it." I appreciated that the teachers had found a way to call the child out for hitting without Adrian somehow getting made fun of for "tat-tling." I also wondered how this could have been happening without the teachers seeing it, at least one of the times. My heart was heavy and I wondered if I could have done something so that Adrian would have come to me after the first time the boy hit him, not after repeated punches.

To me, it was no coincidence that Adrian first spoke about being hit when we were having a great time during a Sunday brunch with Hope, an African American lesbian friend who, like Adrian, was born and raised in New York City. She had begun talking about a poster she had up in her office (as the director of multicultural affairs at a university in New England) that reads, "Sticks and Stones Will Break Your Bones and Words Will Hurt You, Too." Adrian said he knew about that because there was a kid at school who had been hitting him. Hope asked him what he did about it and Adrian said, "Nothing." Hope said, "That's no good." Hope and I began trying to get the details — no easy task since Adrian quickly became monosyllabic. We learned enough to know that I would go to the teachers straight away on Monday. And I saw again, that as with Christopher, there were things that Adrian could talk about and get support for with African American people he trusted that could not happen with me alone. With the dean of admissions, the counselor, the teacher, and a friend, I had been there, permitted to witness the telling, the lesson. But there is no way a white woman can raise an African American child alone. The politics of race and gender and class reign.

Limb from limb

A WHITE ANTIRACIST POET FRIEND OF MINE writes me a treasured letter, in a time when E-mail and phones make letters infrequent. She writes of much news in her life, and a paragraph about how, in a recent visit together, "my way of walking through the world" somehow taught her something about balance. I read her words, grateful for the support, and surprised that she saw me as "in balance" in my body. It feels like such a struggle to me. Because of the early trauma I lived through and the noise of the world that seems nearly impossible to avoid, I have often felt physically fragmented, even before Adrian came. Now, with a nine-year-old boy who is being all of his ages—sometimes three, sometimes five, sometimes seven—embodiment feels more complicated than ever.

When Adrian first came to live with me, he would often touch my face, memorizing the way it felt, the way infants often do, except that he is nine. He now crawls into my lap while I am reading, wanting me to cuddle him like a baby, telling me, once he gets comfortable, "This is how my mommy used to hold me when I was really, really small." As he roots around for a comfy place inside my arms, I am aware of my soft skin but not-so-cushiony

chest and stomach — a product of my years of running and
rowing crew before Adrian came into my life, a product
of learning how to eat when I am physically hungry, not
when I am trying to find love, comfort, or a distraction
from hard feelings. The tight muscles and little breasts,
earned from years of athletics and healing from an eating
problem, are now liabilities as he pronounces, "I have
never felt breasts as stiff as yours." I laugh, squeeze him,
and worry that yes, my body may not be cushiony enough,
familiar enough for him to ever let his body go, to let his
body relax in my arms.

Adrian came to me an already cuddly child, a warmth
nurtured by his biological mother's, Grace's, many years
of holding and loving him. He came wanting to hug constantly, to sit close, to check in with me physically, on a
regular basis. What a gift that has been for me, since the
touch between us made me feel bonded right away. I have
heard of so many children who have been tossed between
people, in and out of the Department of Social Services,
who have lost the ability to bond physically, who interpret
touch as invasion, not closeness. Since Adrian came, much,
if not most, of our bonding together has been on a physical level. So, this weekend, when he doesn't want hugs
from me for the first time, I panic. He jerks away from my
body, screaming, "I don't want you. I want my mommy."
This reaction follows a call from one of his relatives the
night before when she conveyed an impossible message:
"We want you with us, but we don't have room for you."

The following evening we start to talk, after I had to
physically drag him out of the basement of a theater where
he had run to get away from me, yelling, "I won't hug you.
I won't hug anyone except my family." That night he cries

hard in my arms, burying himself in my warmth, telling me, between the sobs, that he is sorry he yelled at me. He asks me again and again if I am going to beat him for "being so bad in public." I assure him many times that I am not going to beat him—that I just want to understand why he pulled away. What made him so scared? Between sobs, he explains that he was afraid that hugging me would be a sign that he wants to be with me instead of with his biological family. Somehow, a hug from me had gotten caught up in his worry that he was betraying his mother and his grandmother. In his child's mind, he had abandoned his family, not the other way around. My body—a safe haven for him. My body—what he sees as standing in the way of getting to his mother.

Embodiment feels more confusing than I remember it being for a very long time. I slip out of the house in the 5:00 a.m. darkness to go for a run before I wake him for the get-to-school rush of the morning. And I try to remember to breathe, even as academic life sometimes makes me feel like I am teaching in a morgue—as the inertia of bureaucratic process and a turn away from substance by some faculty and administrators wreaks havoc on intellectual thought.

I recently heard that the intellectual quotient of a household decreases by half for each child living in it. I push myself to resist this. I remind myself to talk with Adrian about the cover stories in the *Boston Globe,* to clip out and read with him the recent Derrick Jackson editorial on why, because of Nike's exploitation of factory workers, he and his family do not buy Nike shoes, no matter how much hype and pressure his children come home with. Somehow, embodiment is all caught up in my need for intellectual thought, since being firmly in my body makes me hungry, starving, racing for real analytical conversation, for real emotional exchange. I feel desperate for time for my journal and the scholarly book I had begun before Adrian came and before the semester started. Yet, I am afraid I will have nothing to say, nothing original. I am panicked — panicked that I am slipping into the anti-intellectual environment that I feel all around me. Embodiment. Even on the good days, I struggle for a way to feel at home in my body.

Having Adrian in my life — and trying to stay in my body and help him stay in his as well — touches on so much about race and class and gender and sexuality that I can barely begin to understand even one piece of the process. As I am driving in the seemingly constant rush-hour traffic from Jamaica Plain along Memorial Drive and the Charles River on a clear fall Friday afternoon to get Adrian from school, I see a cluster of signs and demonstrators. Stretching to see the writing on the signs, I hope that their presence is an early indicator of the upcoming thousands of people who are going to protest Chinese leader Jiang Zemin's speech at Harvard on the weekend. I look, anticipating signs supporting the people of Tibet and honoring the brave protesters at Tiananmen Square. As the traffic ekes closer to the people, I begin to decipher a whole other set of banners — "God = AIDS," "Gore is a fag," "Kill all the Fags," and "Gays = Death." My mind reels trying to make sense of these posters: an antigay rally alongside Jiang Zemin's talk? A counterdemonstration against those activists opposed to China's antidemocratic policies?

I can't figure out why these antigay activists are here, but I am horrified. My body remains perfectly still. In the traffic. Alone in my car. Aghast at the hatred. On my way to pick up Adrian, having just had a meal with an African American friend who, in her ten years working with children caught up in the courts and in group "homes," learned of vicious ways that lesbians get creamed in the courts. She cautions me: "Be careful to keep your body to yourself, to keep your body clothed. Keep strict boundaries between Adrian's body and your body. Any innuendo can be used against you." I scan back in my mind, to Adrian climbing into bed with my partner, Hannah, and me—wanting to get in the middle, wanting to be on top—kissing me, kissing Hannah, all of us laughing together.

This is the same child who, two days earlier, had mimicked a vomiting sound when eight-year-old Diana, Hannah's daughter, whispered that her mommy was a lesbian, a gesture that, retrospectively, I think had more to do with our talking about sexuality in general—all of which is "gross" to him at this point in his life—than it did about lesbians per se. Just this week, he pointed to a flyer on the wall at his school that announced "Gay Pride Week at Silver Street School." He seemed just on the verge of asking if I were going to it, but then lost his nerve. He backed away for that particular minute to tell me that his teacher taught him what pink triangles mean. "Because, you know, my teacher, is a lesbian," Adrian says to me, with pride in his voice, a big smile on his face. "That's terrific, Adrian. Thanks for telling me." I smile big inside, having been grateful from day one to know about his teacher. Now, so glad to hear Adrian report it to me with excitement. I ask him to tell me about pink triangles and he does. "That's what gay men and lesbians wear to tell people they are proud," he explains with an everybody-should-already-know-that tone in his voice. I beam inside. "How come triangles?" I ask. Adrian isn't sure, so I tell him about how the Nazis made Jews and others wear triangles during the Holocaust. The Jews had to wear yellow triangles. Jehovah's Witnesses had to wear violet triangles. Gay men were forced to wear pink triangles. "So how come gays and lesbians wear triangles, then, if it was used against them?" Adrian asks. "To reclaim a history. To turn it inside out. It is an act of resistance and solidarity," I explain. I look in Adrian's direction, wondering if my explanation makes any sense or if I should clarify, only to realize the teachable moment has long since passed. Adrian has run off in another direction with some of his classmates.

I see all this—the antigay demonstration, the Gay Pride Week announcement, Adrian's smiling face as he tells me about his lesbian teacher—during the same week that children in Adrian's classroom throw a doll catalogue across the room while they shout, "Yuck! Dolls are for girls! Who wants them?" Meanwhile, Adrian is getting scapegoated at school for "the way he holds his body" by a group of close-knit, fourth-grade white boys who "don't like dolls" and who have all been together at this private school since kindergarten. Adrian, the new kid on the block, the Black, Caribbean-raised child whose white stepfather used to refer to him as his "slave." Whose stepfather taunted and teased him when he caught Adrian playing with his younger sister's toys. Adrian, who came to me with no toys at all, just stories of how his stepfather used to crush his toys or return them to get refunds so he could buy beer or other drugs.

Adrian, who is fully aware of the stigma attached to boys who play with dolls, opts for Beanie Babies instead,

playing with them for hours on end. Among his games is
an imagined family of Beanie Babies, all together — a
mother, a baby brother, and a baby sister, and, of course,
a very protective older brother. Meanwhile, Adrian is
now becoming a disembodied big brother to his younger
brother and sister Adam and Josie, who live with his
mother. After talking with Adam on the phone this week,
when for the first time Adam called out Adrian's name,
Adrian hangs up and wails for a long time. I hold him as
he cries, deep cries. Adrian, now physically separated
from his little brother and sister. Railing against my body,
pounding on my chest, refusing hugs, balling up his fists,
responding to the injuries he is living through in his body,
through my body.

So, I am grateful to be driving down Memorial Drive
alone — in front of, alongside of, and then past the homophobic demonstration. Alone, hoping that with enough
time, even a few minutes to collect myself, to collect the
pieces of my body, those demonstrators might move on.
Alone to collect myself and breathe deeply, to end this
week, trying to keep my body and Adrian's from a world
that sometimes seems bent on destroying us, tearing us
limb from limb, away from each other, one scene at a
time.

Telling, not telling, still hurting

ANDREA CALLED TONIGHT to tell me that she had spoken with her mother, Grace, who has gone back to live with her husband, Damion — the man who had beaten and abused Adrian since he was a baby. Grace told Andrea that she just couldn't stand living in the homeless shelter anymore. Damion had also threatened that if she didn't move back in with him, he would find ways to hurt her and her two youngest children.

I guess I should have thought more before I told Adrian that his mother was no longer in a shelter and was back with Damion. More reflection might have helped me see that giving Adrian that information wouldn't necessarily help him. But it is a difficult line I am trying to walk. I don't want to withhold information from him, so that he learns things about his mother a step at a time. I thought he had probably been worried about her being in a shelter, given the many times he had lived in shelters with her before. And I thought telling him might give him another example of why he would not have been safe staying with her. Had he been with her this fall, he would have had to stay with Damion's relatives in Idaho when Grace traveled to New York to see her family each month. Or Adrian would have needed to go with her and then miss school. Now he would be back living with Damion.

On some level, Adrian must have known that. But when I told him that his mother was back with Damion, he interpreted my telling as being judgmental of her. He said I didn't have any idea how hard life was for her. "Don't you know," he accused me, "that the shelter is no place to live and that she was doing the right thing by going back home? Don't you know that my mother had to be with Damion for financial reasons and since Adam and Josie are Damion's children also?"

When I said that I didn't think living with Damion was her only option, or a safe one, he turned the conversation to how ungenerous I was being by not asking his mother to live here with us. He told me with simple clarity, "Mommy and the two kids could have my room and you and I could get bunk beds to sleep in your room." To me, what was amazing about his plan is how he somehow arranged it that he and I would be together, while his mother and two younger siblings would be together. I was left wondering if he is starting to feel connected to me, or if he put the two of us together because he feels pushed out by his mother. It is probably a little bit of both. Either way, I am the bad guy in his head—either falsely judging his mother or refusing to care for her—while he accepts what he sees as her version of the situation completely.

What part of the story do I tell?

ADRIAN COMES UP TO MY STUDY to ask me if I like the new airplane he has made with his Legos. I praise the sleek yellow, black, and silver air glider he is flying around the room. As I watch him, I wish silently that he would stick with Legos and Beanie Babies rather than his recent acquisition — action figures. All fall he asked for action figures, which, naive childless person that I have been, I assumed were simply figures that could move. So, when Christmas came, I told people of his request, which meant that he was given three action figures, each gruesome in its own way.

Modeled after ultramasculine, muscle-bound cartoon characters — Spiderman, Batman, and the Hulk — these nine-inch plastic dolls are all based on concepts of restriction, bondage, and instant liberation. All three look like a cross between a sumo wrestler and a gorilla, with muscles only developed by those who lift weights during all their waking hours. The Hulk figure, arguably the worst of the lot, comes bound to a huge cementlike block that looks like a combination Nautilus weight-lifting machine and electric chair. The instructions show Adrian that he is supposed to strap the Hulk in at the legs, arms, torso, and neck and then push a button on the back, which allows Hulk to burst out of his bondage. I shudder as Adrian shows me how Hulk should be strapped in, flashing on Mumia Abu-Jamal, on death row in Pennsylvania, and my friend David Gilbert, who is in prison until 2056 for his militant organizing against imperialism and racism in the 1960s and 1970s.

The "waiting area" at the prison in rural upstate New York where David is held is furnished with three rows of long-since-faded yellow and red Formica counters. To the right of the dead yellow tables is a floor-to-ceiling photograph of a grassy courtyard lined with rows of flowers, plants, and neatly sculptured walkways. Against this photograph, prisoners are allowed to have their pictures taken with a visitor. To the side of this mural is an old, paint-chipped wooden chair with tall legs and a straight back, which has been placed on top of a wooden block. Andrea, who came with me this time to visit David, takes one look at the chair and says, "An electric chair. I guess to remind us who has the power, huh?"

The night before I drove to the prison, Adrian gave me a letter he had written after I told him I was going to visit a friend. Adrian wanted to know why I was going to the prison and why David was there. I told him David is an antiracist activist who is in prison because of his militancy against racism. "Like Martin Luther King?" Adrian asked. "Well, kind of," I said, "but more like Malcolm X," I reminded him from a book we recently read, "who supported the struggle against racism by any means necessary."

Before I kissed Adrian good-bye, he gave me his letter with a stern warning that I absolutely could not open it until I crossed the New York border. I put on my most

sad and dejected face until he said, "Well, okay, you can
read it now and then again when you get to New York."
So I read it out loud to him, my eyes filling with tears. He
wrote: "How are you doing with your friend? I printed
this for you and you are still and always will be in my
heart. Am I in yours? Well I love you and you are very nice
and kind hearthed [*sic*]. I love you bye." I hugged him
and kissed him all over his face, feigning an attempt to eat
his ears (a game we began when he first came), and I told
him that of course he was in my heart, right at the center.
He asked if I was going to end up in prison like David, for
standing up for what I believe in, and I said no, I was not,
that I was on a different path from David, even though
I admire his courage to try to do right.

I started the journey from Boston to New York on my
own, planning to meet Andrea and Ella, the woman I had
been long-term partners with when I first met Andrea. The
plan was that I would drive west on the Massachusetts
Turnpike as they drove north from Connecticut to the Pike
until we met up, so that Andrea could then drive with me
the rest of the way to the prison to meet David for the
first time. After two hours of driving in the dark in a terrible snowstorm (so we could get there by 9:30 A.M., before
"count" — the time each day when all prisoners must be
in their cells so they can be counted), I realized that my
little bottom-of-the-line Honda Civic simply wouldn't
make it in the Berkshires in this weather. After spinning
out twice, I called Ella on her car phone to admit that I
would not be able to drive the rest of the way. Ella, in her
red Saab and with her three decades of driving in the
snow, offered to drive Andrea and me to the prison once
I met up with them on the Pike.

What part of the story do I tell?

We finally arrive at the prison, exhausted from driving in the blinding snow. We keep our eyes like steel as the correctional officer behind the computer assumes that, as a white woman, I am separate from Ella and Andrea, both of whom are Black, even though we came in together. I inform him with a cold and formal voice that we are, indeed, together and have been. We keep our bodies tight as they search us far more carefully than they have when I have come alone. Another guard assigns us to sit in chairs directly next to other visitors, even though there are plenty of empty seats that day, which, had we been assigned them, would have given everyone more privacy.

The correctional officer finally escorts David to the visitors' area. David, as always, quickly begins by asking questions about the drive and the holidays, as is his nature, to put the focus on others before himself. Soon, I am marveling at Andrea's openhearted and astute conversation with David. She wants to know how he organizes across race in prison, about the relationship between the Black Liberation Army and the Weather Underground, about how David negotiates living in the all-male culture in the prison. She tells him about how the Formica counters in the visitors' area are right out of welfare and emergency health care offices in New York City. Counters from offices where she had sat countless hours as a child while she accompanied her mother to get food stamps. David and Andrea talk about how the same class and race of people are sitting in this room and in those welfare offices in the city. David answers her questions carefully, deliberately, and with the passion of someone who understands what Cherríe Moraga and Gloria Anzaldúa refer to as "theory in the flesh" — teaching through the experiences we are living through in our bodies.[1]

David asks Andrea what she thinks about Steven Spielberg's new film *Amistad*. It turns out neither of them has seen it yet, but David has read some reviews. He talks about how some of the reviewers say that *Amistad* falls into the same trap as *Glory* and *Driving Miss Daisy*, portraying white people as the real heroes, despite overwhelming evidence to the contrary. David also tells Andrea about the connection between the film's story and George Jackson's defense when he was on trial in California. Defending his actions, Jackson had evoked the *Amistad* decision, which granted a "slave the right to revolt." I look at these two sitting across from each other. She, a young Trinidadian-born woman who, until now, had never heard of George Jackson and who is now learning a piece of civil rights history from a middle-aged white man whose measured protests in prison include passing history down to his almost-grown son, the young men who come to prison, and now Andrea. He passes on a critique of a film that puts white people at the center, while he embodies a history that makes room for white justice seekers.

We leave the prison a few hours later — always too soon, always with my tears — and I feel as torn up as I have after other visits. Followed by the image of the fake bucolic mural, the sullenness of the correctional officers, the stark light of the bare light bulbs in the visitors' room, the filthy bathroom in the visitors' area, the electric chair standing as an evil witness just to our right, as David, Andrea, Ella, and I try to talk calmly and with humor about our lives.

What part of the story do I tell?

The critical race theorist Mari Matsuda writes that theory is based on dialogue about contradictions that play themselves out in the body.[2] Feeling at war in my body, as one part drives away from the prison and another remains behind, I ask Ella, who knows me so well, why I feel so torn apart when I leave the prison. Of course, there are many obvious reasons. It is all outrageous. David, who is struggling for the basic right to eat only food that will not make him sick. A misdiagnosed illness a year and a half ago followed by poorly prescribed medication caused him to develop a bad allergy to all forms of wheat, so that eating just a little wheat leaves him with chronic fatigue–like symptoms. He has requested a wheat-free diet multiple times, to almost no avail. David, who is organizing a model AIDS education program whose success means he will likely continue to be assigned to one of the three worst prisons in New York. David, who has recently been denied what is almost always granted to prisoners — the right to a deathbed visit with his mother, who is in her eighties and has had severe health problems. David, who has never received a disciplinary violation, is still perceived as too much of a threat to the system to obtain a visit with his mother or a wheat-free diet, as his charisma, sensitive manner, perseverance, and antiracism have allowed him to organize across race and religion in prison since 1981 and into the future.

These reasons, which Ella and Andrea and I chronicle together, explain why leaving the prison each time I see him makes me feel so small, so vulnerable, so weakened by the harshness all around me. But after Andrea and Ella meet him for the first time and are able to see him with me, and me with him, they help me see another dimension to my reaction—that there is another reason for my intense connection, my full-body response to visits with him. Ella turns to me in the car and says, "Well, he could be your twin. Look at the way he uses his hands—totally animated when he is speaking about AIDS education, multiracial organizing, the latest book he has reviewed. His gestures are so Jewish. So full of life." Gestures he no doubt learned as a kid and I must have learned during my eight years studying at Brandeis University. Gestures I first noticed when my graduate school mentor and friend, Issac Berman, a dignified patriarch at Brandeis, first pointed my hand movements out to me and said, "See, you are part Jewish. Look how you talk with your hands." Ella says to me, "Look at how David uses his eyes—intense, confirmed, direct, passionate—just like you when you are really involved in conversations." And, Ella explains, "He has an androgynous-looking body. So much like you." My body, which is the spitting image of my father's body, who is now dead, who was also named David, who, like this David, had the soul of a poet.

"Look," Ella tells me, "look at what David stands for. Look at the validation and guidance he can give you. You and he are among the white people who see the madness of racism and are working to change that. Look, you know that you could be him. He could be you. In another place and time." I begin to disagree, citing my fear of guns, my fear of violence, my worry that violence just begets more violence, but Ella interrupts. "It is hard to comprehend now," she says, "the sense of possibility that we were all living with in the sixties, the sense that struggling hard, even being willing to give up your life, would amount to something, could conceivably change the world."

In the 1990s, it *is* hard for me to understand why David had been so convinced that militancy was necessary. The meditator in me, the person who deliberately and proudly chose a school founded on principles of nonviolence for Adrian, has a hard time picturing me, now or thirty years ago, deciding to make bombs and carry guns. But, as Ella said, it is impossible to really know what I would have done at that time. In the late 1960s, a small group of white people were making principled arguments about why — when African Americans were being gunned down on the streets and risking their lives for change — white people were obligated to take those risks as well. Their logic was that white skin privilege could afford them a way into the banks, libraries, and courts, where they needed to obtain the money, guns, and legal information necessary to support the movement. White revolutionaries, as they called themselves, could serve as decoys. White revolutionaries would show through their actions that, yes, there were white people who were passionate about justice. Who did not go along with the vicious dogs and the police who had trained them, the church-burning vigilantes, the business-as-usual politics of segregated lives and public policy.

For the book I am working on about white antiracist activism, I recently interviewed Jaye Stein, the director of a multiracial women's activist group in Albany, who was also in the Weather Underground with David. During the interview, Jaye talked of the irony and absurdity of living forty miles apart from David on the same road — both on Route 4 in upstate New York. She lives in a ranch house with her chiropractor partner and their son, with a swimming pool and a big front yard. David is in one of the three "burn circuit" prisons of the twenty-nine prisons in New York State. Jaye spoke of how she could have been him. He could have been her.

But it didn't occur to me until Ella prodded that I could be David. Had I been David, though, I don't believe I could have done what he has done. I don't think I could have survived. The house I dreamed of repeatedly as a child — what dream interpreters refer to as a person's psychic house — was an abandoned mental institution that I could not escape. I remember when I was a teenager, sitting on the front porch of my house and playing guitar, trying to memorize songs so that I would have them to keep me company if I were ever in prison. I couldn't have told you why I assumed I would need songs in prison, why I would be in prison at all. I didn't ask myself those questions. I just knew I should memorize the songs then, while I had the sheet music in front of me.

When Ella said that David could be my twin, I looked at her in amazement. Amazed by her quick-fire, accurate insight. Grateful that she knew me so well that she could put into words what had been bumping around miserably in my body. Aware that I couldn't have diagnosed the connection myself. I am far too critical of all that I haven't done. I am far too aware of how insignificant my own work for justice has been to see myself as David in another time. But with her confidence in me, and her quick naming before I could deny it, I knew that what she said felt right. Yes, David is the first twin I have ever felt. The first person I could call my twin is in prison, with no chance of parole until the middle decade of the twenty-first century. This smart man, this principled man whom many, many

people come to visit in a room furnished with fake yellow
Formica counters and a wooden electric chair, quite possibly the same vintage as the one many are now planning to
use to execute Mumia Abu-Jamal. David, who recently
wrote to me that he has reduced a thirty-page article on his
life and struggle against racism to a simple haiku: "Love for
the people/means nonstop struggle against/imperialism."[3]

I come home from the prison to Adrian and Christmas.
To his new Legos set. To his explaining Hulk to me and
why, of all the things he got for Christmas, he likes the
action figures most. That makes sense in a way. Muscular,
male figures who are able to break out of seemingly
impossible situations, even electric chairs. Adrian comes
to ask me if I like the airplane he has just made from Legos
and I say, "Yes, yes." And I think to myself, I like the
Legos. I like the Beanie Babies, and your love for the
dogs, and your impulse to go to the laptop and write
whenever you are upset. And I think to myself, what piece
of this story about David do I tell him? What piece of the
story about Mumia Abu-Jamal and Leonard Peltier do I
tell him? When and how do I tell him that "Hulk" simply
won't do? What piece of this story can his beautiful brown
eyes take in? Now? Later? In pieces? What do I need to
do so that David Gilbert and Mumia Abu-Jamal and
Leonard Peltier and the hundreds of other political prisoners can be on the outside, teaching Adrian what it means
to be gentle, principled men?

I rest my head in my hands. I look up at Adrian and
wonder what life will bring him. I time travel between my
house and the prison, across the snow, through the walls.
When I wrote David to tell him that I had begun to mother

Adrian, David responded that it was only when he became a father that he really became an adult. I am left wondering if being an adult means accepting that alone, I am insufficient to the task of finding answers to my questions.

Heart on the table, in my hands

I HAVE AN HOUR AND A HALF before I go to Bob the Chef's, a soul food restaurant in the South End in Boston, to celebrate with the African American studies faculty the change from program to department status at the college where I teach. Soon, it will be one of the few departments of African American studies at small liberal arts schools in the United States — a major leap forward in giving African American studies faculty hiring autonomy and the room to build a cohesive curriculum. Adrian is with his chosen aunt and uncle, Kerry and Kayode, for the night. I have chocolate chips and chai tea, a deep-blue lit candle, and blessed quiet in the house.

It has been such an emotional time these last several months. As a consequence of mothering Adrian, I am going through my childhood again, sorting through memories, as if for the first time, that I thought I had already resolved through my eight years of therapy. I am seeing ways I react toward Adrian that I never thought I would see. Many behaviors that I thought belonged to others — what other people did to me or what I did and then left behind me — are clearly still alive inside of me.

Sometimes I hate what I see in myself. Mainly how angry I am capable of getting. How much I want to grab Adrian and force him to do things sometimes. Last night, I did grab him and try to force him onto his bed after he had refused, several times, to listen to me. He responded by pushing back. Early on, I remember getting into physical situations with him — of my holding him still — when he would try to run out of the house or run away from me when I was talking with him. There have also been times when he would flail and wail in my arms as I held him tight, telling him I would not, will not let him go. Last night seemed somewhat different, I guess because *I* was the angry one and he lashed out at me.

When that happened, I started screaming at him, "You astound me. Where do you get off?" I heard myself saying these words as I was screaming at myself, "What are you doing? You are acting just like your mother used to act sometimes. Violent. Out of control. Irrational." In that moment, I hated myself. Thankfully, the exchange was momentary. Thankfully, I knew to leave the room. I went out into the cold air with the three dogs and knew again what people mean by the winter air clearing your head. It didn't clear my head exactly, but it gave me enough of a breath to go in and talk, and, as it turned out, talk and talk and talk with Adrian.

I didn't say I was sorry for trying to force him into bed. Maybe I should have or still should. But I did explain that I get extremely frustrated when I have to say things over and over again, basic things — brush your teeth, get into bed — sometimes with him not answering me at all. Sometimes with him whining, negotiating, just not doing it. Now

I think about the scene and I can't understand what exactly made me so angry. Why I started to feel like I was going to lose it. But I was there—in an out-of-control place—and I hate that.

When I explained to Adrian how frustrated I sometimes get, he said that he deserved to be punished. He said that he had been disobedient and that parents have the right to get very angry at their children. "If you want to beat me now, you should," Adrian said. "I deserve it." I told him that I wasn't angry at him anymore. That I wasn't about to beat him. He told me that he had bumped his head on the headboard at some point in our exchange and that it really hurt. I felt the back of his head. No bump. But in a way that didn't matter. His lashing back made more sense to me once I realized that he'd bumped his head. Even though I didn't do it deliberately, he must have been scared and angry when he got hurt. That somehow relieved me. I realized that he didn't lash out just because I had pushed him onto the bed, but also because he had gotten hurt. I began rubbing his head, telling him I wasn't mad, that I was sorry that his head hurt. Then we both began to cry. And cry. And cry.

I wondered then if that was the "right" thing—to let him see me cry. To let him comfort me while I comforted him. I have tried so hard to establish a parent-child relationship with him that is not equal. He is not, and won't be asked to be, my caretaker. He is not in charge or responsible for my emotional well-being. I worried that lying there together, both of us crying, might send a message to contradict the careful weeks and months I had spent letting him know I am the parent and he the child. But my tears were free flowing. And some part of me was so tired of being the brave one. Of him only seeing me in control and in charge and sure of myself.

I didn't entirely understand my tears in that moment. And I still don't. Partly, I think I was grieving for the times my mother hit me. The bald spots, as my sister said, when my mother pulled my hair out, or my sister's hair out. All the times I raised myself. Held myself. Held my sister, Jasmine. Felt alone. Watching her break the bedroom door, putting her hand through the panel of wood. Watching her throw dishes. A whole set. Her going after Jasmine, shaming me.

I don't remember her ever comforting me after those storms. Maybe she did, but I have no memory of it. She was a single mother too much of the time when I was a kid, no doubt feeling even more overwhelmed than I do now. What did she do after those storms? I have not thought about that. Asking her these questions now, when I am thirty-eight and she is fifty-eight, might be a way for us to connect as adults. Somehow, though, I feel such rage, such emptiness. I don't know if I am willing to be vulnerable with her about how hard it is for me to be a parent sometimes.

I never thought I would, as an adult, feel the degree of rage and vulnerability I sometimes feel. Especially now, at thirty-eight. Somehow, I felt I had worked that violence out of my system once I acknowledged and dealt with how out-of-control I got when I first began caring for children (other than my brother and sister). When I was twelve years old, I was asked to accompany a family on their vacation to an island in Canada, serving as the

nanny for their one-year-old and three-year-old. Their
mother, the wife of a well-to-do doctor in the town where
I went to junior high school, left me to get up with her
infant night after night when the child woke for a feeding.
I remember feeding him bottles. Changing him. And
then wishing, hoping, and eventually getting desperate
when he wouldn't go back to sleep, when I couldn't get
him back to sleep. Sometimes I got desperate when he kept
crying after he was dry and fed. As he cried and cried,
I couldn't figure out what to do to make him stop. Sometimes I would shake him, and, I think, pinch him. Yell at
him. Scream at him. His mother and father, who were
sleeping in a whole other wing of the house, were too far
away to be bothered by him or me, or to even know he
and I were in trouble. I don't know how I would eventually calm him after that. I remember nothing of how
I would get myself back to sleep afterward. I know I felt
bad. Ashamed. Feelings that I carried around for years
until, as an adult, I began to see that I was set up. I was
twelve years old and deserved to sleep through the night.
I should never have been saddled with that responsibility.
I had been exploited. Used. I came to hate that child.

At the end of the six-week trip, the family opted not to
pay me. Instead, they gave me a watch and a photo album
of the summer vacation. One picture is of me, with long
skinny legs and long blond hair, standing by a bonfire with
the children close. In another photo I am playing guitar,
with kids all around me. In still another photo, I am wearing a knit, horizontally striped shirt that I had bought for
the trip in case I had to dress up for some fancy occasion.
I was wearing the shirt pulled over a skirt in front of some

government building in Canada. I remember feeling fat in that outfit, thinking that there was something wrong with me, as big as I was getting (or thought I was getting), so much taller than my mother and sister. So much bigger and fatter than they were. It was during that summer that I first remember not letting myself eat during the day, and then sneaking food in the night when hunger would win out over willpower. I remember that the woman of the house, the children's mother, told me that, yes, it might be good if I could lose some weight, and yes, it seemed like I might have put on a few pounds over the summer. I remember feeling ashamed of myself, my size, how big I felt in those horizontal stripes in the picture that day.

The beginnings of an eating problem that I mostly hid and that tore me apart through high school and college. Certainly not starting that summer. More likely starting when my mother's lover began molesting me. He was with my mother that summer, no doubt one reason she was glad to see me take that job. One reason, no doubt, that I don't remember getting a letter from my mother that summer. It wasn't until I was an adult, way into my twenties, that I started to ask myself, who was advocating for me in that situation? Why didn't my mother say, "Hey, you have no right to work my daughter that hard and then not even pay her." Looking back, it makes sense that it didn't even occur to me to talk with someone about what I was doing to that infant, who I continued to take care of for years after I returned home, but whose name I can't, to this day, retrieve.

I put the watch and photograph album away, along with the memories of my abuse of that child, until I sorted through some of it, I thought all of it, in my twenties. I tried to make sense out of that summer before I was a mother, when long-term therapy started to teach me what it was like to have someone watch after me. We started over in many ways. My therapist gave me a teddy bear I could hold in the night. She gave me a birthday gift every year as I cried and cried and cried, wondering if I ever got gifts as a child. I probably did but I have no memory. I remember my therapist walking me twice from one office, where we had met every week for four years, to another, before the construction of the second office was even done. She knew that, given the shape I was in, even her moving just across the way might shake me up.

By then, I had already lived in twenty-five houses in my life. Too many changes. Almost nothing to hold on to as a child except my sister, whom I held on to every night, night after night, my legs wrapped around hers, until early adolescence, when the molestation began. When the molestation drove us apart. A secret that we never told each other or anyone else. A secret that drove us apart. As I was being abused, I felt sure that she was not being abused. As she was being abused, she probably didn't think it was happening to me. My mother didn't know it was happening to either of us.

I lay on Adrian's bed, half on, half off really, and cried and cried. I didn't and wouldn't have explained to him that many reasons for my tears were from the past. I wouldn't have wanted him to carry that burden. But somehow the comfort I got from crying alongside him made it impossible for me to get up, even if maybe it wasn't right for him to see me cry so hard. I cried for getting beaten up. I cried for having no childhood. I cried for losing control as an adult, or worrying that I would lose control, after I thought

I had already worked that through—gotten it out and moved beyond it after mistreating the infant when I was twelve. I had thought that acknowledging that I was capable of being violent toward someone dependent on me had cured me of that reaction. I said none of this to Adrian. There were just tracks from my tears as I held him, he held me, and we cried.

Then we start to talk. Heavy talk. Heartfelt talk. Talk that we may circle around, revisit, talk about again for years and years to come. I ask him if he worries that I will stop caring for him. I ask if he wonders if I will get so angry some day that I will stop loving him. He half-answers a weak "yes," and then, a full-force, plaintive, "How come my mother sent me away? Was I too much for her? How come Adam and Josie get to stay and I am here, away from them? What is wrong with me that I can't be with my real family?" I tell him that he is perfect as he is, not wanting to contradict his accurate, his frighteningly accurate, perception that I think Grace *did* send him away because he was too much for her. He is too smart. Too perceptive. Too caring. Too talkative. Too clear that he needs to learn a lot, see a lot, meet a lot of people. He had become big enough physically that she may have begun to worry that he might start fighting back when Damion hit him. He had become too old for her to take in and out of school, to take from shelter to hotel, to Damion's house, to another shelter, in and out, in and out, time and time again. Adrian was absolutely right about why Grace had asked me to care for him. He was "too much." And that is exactly what makes him amazing. A blessed child. A perfect match for me. A child I bonded with immediately.

As Adrian and I hold each other in the dark, he begins unloading worries and pain that I believe he has been holding on to for a long time. He whispers to me, "You wouldn't believe how hard it is for me to be the darkest kid in my family. I am darker than my mother. Darker than Andrea. Way darker than Josie and Adam, the chosen ones." I hold him tight, whispering back, "You are gorgeous, Adrian. Always have been. Always will be." He turns his face to me again and whispers, "I am scared of every child in my school. I have no friends there." Big tears. Big sobs. Holding me tight. I say with the biggest, most macho voice I can find, "Adrian, if Silver Street School isn't working for you, we will just walk. I am not wedded to that school. We are just checking it out."

He looks at me, pain starting to leave his face, and I continue, "Anywhere you go, there is going to be racism. That is something you — and I — are going to have to deal with anywhere. But if Silver Street School isn't right, someplace else will be better." He says to me, "So, we are basically putting Silver Street on notice?" "Yes," I tell him. "It is our decision, not theirs." Long silence. Still hugging and then, "Well, I want to try one more year, if that is okay." "Well," I remind him, "you are soaring in math and reading. You are very smart. The first year in any new school is hard. Racism makes things hard. We need to keep talking about it as much as we can."

More big silence between the two of us as we continue to hold each other tight, with me half on, half off his bed. Then, "You know, I pushed a kid up against the wall in the boys' bathroom a couple of days ago, and I told him, 'I don't ever want to hear you say that to me again.'" I ask quietly, "What had he done, Adrian? What made you so mad?" More silence from Adrian and then, "I can't remember," clearly unwilling or maybe unable to go the distance in that conversation with me now.

But with his admission, I understand why Adrian has been talking constantly for two days. Why he had to check in with me every seven minutes, all day on Friday, when a snow day meant we were able to be home together. When he pushed the child into the wall, he had done to another a slight version of what Damion had been doing to him for years. My mind races in five directions. If the child had said something cruel or taunting, might Adrian have been right to go after him? On the other hand, even if he had every right to defend himself from what the kid said, it might be Adrian, not the other kid, who would be punished if Adrian were caught. At a school based on nonviolence, his physical response — even if it was a defensive reaction to cruel talk — might well get him in trouble.

I try to explain all of this to Adrian. He says he understands. I am not sure he does. More silence, then I ask, "Did that scare you, Adrian, pushing a child against the wall?" "Not really," Adrian tells me. "He deserved it." I lay low in this part of the conversation, not sure about the next step. I don't want him to act out like Damion had toward him. And yet, I know that Adrian wouldn't have pushed a kid against a wall unless the kid had said something seriously hurtful. Put this part of the conversation on hold, I tell myself. We'll circle back later.

I hug him deep. Pretend to bite his ears. Leave him after his breathing becomes heavy, the breathing he does just before he goes to sleep. I fall into bed. Exhausted. Haunted. Seemingly locked into a past I thought I could leave behind.

So much wanting to do it differently. Followed every day by memories I thought I had sorted through and put on some shelf. Now open drawers. Almost no organization. Heart on the table, in my hands. Trying to forgive myself. Wanting to do right by Adrian.

In the age of no innocence

THE MOST I HAVE DONE SO FAR with my quandary about Adrian's toys, specifically the action figures, is to quietly separate the electric chair/Nautilus machine from its Hulk figure, burying the machine under a bunch of sheets in his closet. (Wondering, is it my place to throw it out? It isn't my toy—it is his. But I don't want him to have it, so it stays in limbo.) So far, Adrian hasn't seemed to notice that the plastic piece that constrains Hulk is missing.

But that grotesque piece of bright pink and lime green plastic keeps calling to me, from underneath the sheets, reminding me of the metaphor Mab Segrest used as the title of her book, *My Mama's Dead Squirrel*.[1] In these essays on lesbian life, racism, literature, and Southern culture, Segrest writes about a dead squirrel her mother found in her living room while entertaining, a smelly dead squirrel that her mother had to either push under the rug or acknowledge openly, in front of the guests. Segrest artfully uses this scene to describe how racism is smack in the middle of family and social gatherings in the South, and elsewhere as well, and that part of her work, as a white woman wanting to defy a racist tradition, is to decide how to successfully discard, rather than ignore, the dead squirrel.

So, on a day when I am supposed to be at my desk, working with life history interviews for my book on anti-racism, I am instead entirely distracted by a piercing noise emanating from under a pile of sheets in Adrian's closet. The noise from the Hulk machine forces me to look up, to take notice, and to make sense of the politics of my silences: what to say and what not to say to Adrian. What does it mean to be a white woman attempting to raise him respectful of African American culture and aware of the violence perpetrated against African American people by people of my race, violence that, I fear, Adrian is already facing?

The fall of our first year together was rough for a number of reasons. Until I could make car-pool arrangements, I was spending three hours a day driving Adrian to and from our mixed-class, multiracial neighborhood in Jamaica Plain through an almost entirely white, middle- and upper-class community to the neighborhood where Silver Street School is located.

People shouldn't drive in Boston. Until Adrian came, I avoided it as much as I could. Drivers in Boston are insane. The protocol, as best as I can tell, is to pretend you don't see anyone around you. Pretend that a car is not driving directly into you as you enter a rotary. Pretend a car is not careening toward you and then crossing in front of you while that car is running a red light. Pretend that the taxi is not literally pushing your bumper, one bump after the next, on Storrow Drive between Boston University and Logan Airport. Before Adrian, I knew that valuing my life meant taking the Green Line subway downtown instead of driving. Riding my bike across the river to crew practice instead of driving. Accepting rides with everybody and anybody who grew up learning to drive in Boston or New York City, instead of southern California, where I learned to drive. Where traffic lights matter. Where crosswalks are recognized. Where pedestrians count. Where there is a lot of traffic, but not insanity.

Given my predilections for life and calm and predictability, these daily three-hour commutes to and from Adrian's school had been a major shock to my system, quickly teaching me why my sister, who has two children in grammar school, has affectionately referred to her van as the "hag wagon" since she began toting them around Los Angeles. Given my constant complaining through the fall, Hannah thought that books on tape might save me from myself, and started me off with a beautifully produced, unabridged edition of Ernest Gaines's novel, *A Lesson before Dying*. Listening to it, all six tapes, all twelve sides, through the snow and sleet of January trips to and from school is the reason why the plastic piece that is supposed to constrain the Hulk is screaming at me, refusing to be covered up by the sheets in Adrian's closet.

A Lesson before Dying revolves around a twenty-one-year-old African American, Jefferson, who lives in New Orleans in the late 1940s on a former plantation. Jefferson just happened to be at the wrong place at the wrong time one afternoon with two of his Black friends, who ended up holding up a white store clerk, shooting him, and then getting shot themselves. Jefferson watched the terrifying scene, stunned out of his senses. In that moment of panic, as all three lay dying on the floor, Jefferson, a bystander, freaked out. He began to run, after he had grabbed a bottle of liquor, though he had never drunk before, and the money in the cash register drawer. The upshot of the night-marish scene is that Jefferson is found guilty of murder and sentenced to die by electrocution in the county jail.

Jefferson's lawyer had urged the all-white jury not to sentence him to death, arguing, with his hand on Jefferson's shoulder, that it made no sense to execute a hog. Not worth it, why bother, he argued unsuccessfully to the jury. Better to let him stay in jail all his life than to execute what was really only an animal. Jefferson's godmother, injured beyond words, was clearly disturbed by the viciousness of the prosecuting attorney, but was more horrified by the defense attorney, who thought he was doing Jefferson a favor by calling him a hog. After the trial, Jefferson's god-mother asked the Black teacher at the one Black school to give Jefferson a lesson before dying — to teach him that he was not a hog, that he was a man. Jefferson's godmother, the woman who loves him the most, calls out to the teacher for help, a plea reminiscent of a verse in Claude McKay's 1922 poem, "If We Must Die":

> *If we must die, let it not be like hogs*
> *Hunted and penned in an inglorious spot*
> *Like men we'll face the murderous cowardly pack*
> *Pressed to the wall, dying but fighting back.*

Jefferson does end up learning the lesson his godmother asks the teacher to teach, to a great extent because of Jefferson's willingness to write, think, and feel his way through the days before the execution.

Especially because I had been transcribing interviews of political prisoners and activists who work with them, I couldn't shake the graphic and outrageous details of the novel during my waking or sleeping hours. Many images

followed me—the contemptuous spirits of the white offi-
cials who supervised the execution, the sinister and
victim-playing tone of the white sheriff's wife, the way in
which the novel could have been set in the 1880s as easily
as in the 1940s or the 1960s. But what dogged me most
was the teacher's decision to tell his grammar school students about Jefferson's trial and impending execution. He
told these students that if they did not learn their reading,
writing, and arithmetic, they would end up like Jefferson.
On the days when the teacher felt he was not able to get
through to Jefferson at all—in the hour sessions he spent
with Jefferson in his cell—the teacher took his anger out
on his students, hitting them with rulers, shaming them
into subservient attention, informing them they were no
better than bugs if they didn't spell right, write straight,
and speak in complete sentences. These young children
were asked to kneel for two hours during the execution—
to show their support for Jefferson.

I found myself feeling sick, so mad at the teacher for
telling the children about the execution, thinking that
there was no reason, at their very young age, to have to
carry the weight of that racist civilization in their bodies.
There has to be some space for innocence. Telling the
children about Jefferson's execution left the burden of
history on their backs too early. And yet, as I wrestled
with this, the burden they carried seemed outrageously
unavoidable.

I deliberately turned off the tapes when Adrian was in
the car. I hid the plastic electric chair/Nautilus machine.
And I thought back to what I knew, to what I was taught
growing up. I grew up listening to the poetry of Nikki
Giovanni and Langston Hughes, poetry my mother read to

me while passing on her passion for truth-telling words.
I remember my mother singing a song to me, "Ode to Billy
Joe," which, as I remembered it, was about a woman who
jumped off the Tallahatchie Bridge in Mississippi. I remember wondering if my mother wanted to do that too. If that
is why she sang that song to me. I remember her reading
me the line, "The buzz saw snarled and rattled in the
yard," from "Out, Out—," a poem by Robert Frost about
a little boy whose arm is accidentally sawed off by a buzz
saw. That itself was horrible. What was even worse,
though, is that the community hardly notices. Frost
writes,

> No one believed. They listened at his heart.
> Little — less — nothing! — and that ended it.
> No more to build on there. And they, since they
> Were not the one dead, turned to their affairs.

I am not sure of all that I felt about that poem as a
child, the songs my mother sang, those realities. As an adult
I have felt of two minds, appreciative that my mother ex-
posed me to the rhythm and depth of poetry so early, some
of which I am now reading to Adrian. I remember thinking that hearing those heavy poems when I was so young
must have meant I was smart. At the same time, I have
wondered about my mother giving me so much so young,
for my thinking I was somehow responsible for the injustice, somehow trapped in a civilization I was too young to
change or make sense of.

Now, raising Adrian, I recoil when the African American
teacher begins educating the children about Jefferson's
sentence. I cry out inside, "Don't do that. They are too

young. It is too much." And I did shut off the tape when Adrian was in the car, only now wondering if we should have listened to it together.

Last night, as Adrian and I watched the news on TV, a particularly pink-faced, white reporter smiled at the end of his segment about tonight's scheduled execution of Karla Faye Tucker, who will be the first woman executed in Texas since the Civil War. Adrian noticed the reporter's totally unnecessary smile and commented, with pain in his voice, that the smile was cruel. Marita Golden, in *Saving Our Sons*, describes how she and other African American mothers worry that they are raising targets.[2] She writes about conversations with Joyce Ladner, the eminent sociologist and former vice president at Howard University, who sent her African American son to a boarding school for high school. Her decision wasn't so much about a private school education and certainly not because she didn't want his company. Rather, she wanted him to be alive to graduate from high school.[3]

This weekend, Adrian and one of his Indian–African American eight-year-old friends went exploring at the construction site across the street from our house only to run home, totally breathless, telling me, with gasping breaths, about how two teenagers — one Black and one white — chased them away, screaming dirty epithets, scaring them back "into their place." So who am I protecting, except myself, by turning off the audiotape of *A Lesson before Dying* when Adrian is with me? So much I need to know. I feel wobbly in the knees, wanting so much to be up to the task, looking to those around me for help, overwhelmed when I can't find it.

This week, Adrian brought home an assignment that involved writing an essay about a scene the teachers had "made up." The paragraph read:

> *Lydia is a nine-year-old girl who lives with her grand-mother and grandfather, sisters, mother, and father in a house in Jamaica Plain. Although her street is getting safer, her mother still doesn't let her play outside at night. Lydia goes to a public school attended by Black and Latino students where there are thirty-two students per teacher. The school doesn't have money for everyone to have their own books or desks so they share.*

The questions the teachers asked Adrian to answer in essay form were: What forms of racism is Lydia experiencing now? And what forms is she likely to face in the future? Adrian was dumbfounded. I felt overwhelmed. Then angry. Then furious. Then speechless. I saw firsthand what Patricia Williams writes about in *The Alchemy of Race and Rights: Diary of a Law Professor*. In this powerful book, Williams tracks how law school assignments often require students of color and gay men and lesbians to write against themselves. In order to get the answers "right," they have to accept as a given the stereotype of gay people as carriers of AIDS, African American men as perpetrators of violence, and poor people as welfare cheats. What may, on the surface, appear to be an objective assignment requires accepting lies that are rarely named.

As I turned to Adrian's assignment, my mind spinning in a downward spiral, I caught myself beginning to take my anger out on him, as he dawdled, thought of every reason to get up and not work, ate three clementine oranges, begged to watch cartoons, and asked me to write the essay for him. On the surface, perhaps the assignment seems positive. The teachers were responding to Martin Luther King Day by introducing a series of spelling words that all children should know — racism, equality, injustice, and the like — which the teachers then wanted the children to use in context. But Adrian told me that so far all they had talked about at school was all the good work Martin Luther King had accomplished.

From what Adrian remembered, the students had not yet had a lesson about how racism is institutionally enforced. They had not talked about the trick of whiteness that leads people to think that racism takes place only where the Black and Latino children go to school, where the Black and Latino children live. I was left wondering, why was the assignment about racism set in Jamaica Plain? Why not at Silver Street School? Given the scenario in the assignment, all Adrian could surmise was that racism occurred because African American and Latino children attended Lydia's school. In addition, Adrian was asked to identify the racism in the story even though its clues suggested that it would be impossible to answer the question without talking about class.

Without an initial conversation about how Adrian and other African American youth might not be safe on *any* street — Brookline, Newton, or Jamaica Plain — Adrian was left thinking that Jamaica Plain isn't safe because Black and Latino people live here. So, we talked. About tax structures and how property values determine the tax base that funds the schools and how suburban children get twice the education dollars per head that children in the city do. We talked about police brutality against Blacks and Latinos in Brookline, the South End, and Newton — white towns, mixed-race towns, wealthy and poor towns. We talked about how differences in police surveillance partly explain why we lock the car doors when we park on the street in Jamaica Plain and sometimes not in a residential driveway in Brookline. We talked about how that is about race and class.

An hour later, I realize that I am still part of the problem as Adrian says to me, "With all this talk about racism, I begin to feel bad that I am Black." I gulp. I cry inside and gasp for air, for a way to help him shift the blame away from himself and onto white institutions. Hoping that an analogy about sexuality that I have used before to bridge gaps between us will work again, I say, "Adrian, just because there is homophobia directed at me because I am a lesbian doesn't mean I should stop being a lesbian, right?" "What kinds of homophobia?" he wants to know.

"Well," I tell him, hoping that the parallels will be close enough to make sense to him, "homophobia in the form of not feeling comfortable in certain neighborhoods, of not being able to get legally married or adopt children as an out lesbian." He wiggles in his chair as I continue. "Homophobia," I tell him, "such as getting my bike tires slashed at a gay rights demonstration. Someone putting a disgusting chicken foot on my windshield at Brandeis University after I had finished a talk there on trauma and recovery among lesbian and heterosexual African American, Latina, and white women. Seeing my name dug out on a poster announcing a talk I was doing at the University of Massachusetts on multicultural education." I ask Adrian, "The problem is with homophobia, not me, right?" He agrees, wanting to know more about the disgusting chicken foot, true to his nine-year-old sense of humor. With each example of homophobia I give him, his face scrunches up more as he says, "That just isn't fair." But I see my analogy isn't enough. And he sees it, too, quietly informing me that, "Well, not everyone knows you are a lesbian. Everyone always knows I am Black."

I look at his sweet face, his gorgeous long eyelashes, and then come back to the assignment, realizing another part of the problem. Embedded in the assignment — in the scene about Lydia's family — is an assumption that everything is being done *to* Lydia and her family. There is nothing in the question or our answer so far that leaves room for their struggle, their resistance, their community activism, or their community pride. So I tell Adrian that even though we have done the paragraphs the assignment required, we need to add another paragraph about how Lydia and her family fight back.

We brainstorm together about how this fictitious family might be part of a larger group invested in making the neighborhood safe and the schools accountable to their children. We surmise that they might be part of a neighborhood block association. Perhaps one of the parents teaches at the school. And we talk some more about racism at Silver Street School. I try to explain why, while Adrian faces racism at the school, I still think it is a better place for him than a Boston public school. He looks me straight in the face and asks, "But they are all Black and Latino in Boston, right?" "Yes, they are," I say. "I would prefer you to go to a school with many, many more children of color. But then there is the issue of funding, of the teacher-student

ratio, and of the danger on the streets of Boston...."
I drone on.

Too many lessons before dying. Too many lessons while I am trying to help Adrian live, breathe freely, stay open with his head high on the street and at home. It all makes me rethink my adult ambivalence about hearing "Ode to Billy Joe" and Robert Frost's buzz saw poem as a child.

Maybe there are no children here any more, if the truth be told about the violence surrounding us in this society. Adrian's early childhood was taken from him when he was one year old by his stepfather, a white man who beat him mercilessly. His stepfather repeatedly told Adrian that the Bible said that parents should beat their children when they are naughty. Adrian was in foster care a year ago at this time, after his stepfather was arrested.

Still, I wonder whether I should turn the tape of *A Lesson before Dying* on or off when Adrian gets in the car. He's four feet, eleven and a half inches tall. He's grown three and a half proud inches since August, in the six months we have been together. Tall enough to be one of the older children in the grammar school in Ernest Gaines's novel. I am still unsure whether Adrian and I should be listening to the novel together now or in a couple of years. On the other hand, the plastic electric chair/Nautilus machine under the sheets in the closet, I am now sure, has got to go. In the trash, with no mention to Adrian as I try to silence one screeching voice in the cacophony of voices that I carry around with me now.

Once I catch my breath from the preaching and teaching required to do the homework assignment with Adrian, I can hear some calm silence around me. I'll make an appointment to talk with the teachers, both white, both caring, both wanting, I believe, to do right by Adrian and issues of race. In that meeting, which I dread, which I could easily put off, I will try to talk about my concerns while avoiding a holier-than-thou tone with them that can only make matters worse. I need to somehow talk with them, a white woman to two white women, about how we can all be part of a solution. I need to explain how I see these problems in the assignment and see myself as part of the problem, too. I somehow need to come to that conversation without my rage, while still holding them and myself accountable for moving beyond the liberal conceptions of race that allow them, and me, to make racism a problem that happens "where the Black children live." I reach for the words of Maureen Reddy and Jane Lazarre — two white women who wrestle with what racial integrity means for us as we try to raise Black children.[4] I spend a passionate and intense morning in a café with Delilah, an African American woman preacher and single parent of a seventh-grade boy at Silver Street School, who has been talking with the teachers and administrators there far longer than I have. She validates what I see, and reminds me to choose my battles as she explains why, despite the troubles, the school is still a better place for her son than other schools in the area.

Lost time, in time, on time, with time

HAVING SEEN THE TITLE OF THIS BOOK on my desk, Adrian turns to me, seemingly out of the blue, at the breakfast table and asks, "If what you are writing is called 'Mothering without a Compass,' does that mean you don't know what you are doing?"

A quick easy laugh comes out of my body with a big smile. So smart he is. So quick. So to the point. I take a big breath while, inside, two opposite answers in equally clear voices chant to each other: "Of course, I know what I am doing. No, I definitely don't know what I am doing. I am winging it." Closer to the truth, I think to myself, "Well, I don't know what I am doing. I have never done this before. I am going a day at a time." At the same time, I remind myself not to say that to him. He needs to feel my confidence. Confidence I do have, intuitively, somehow.

With various answers spinning rapidly through my mind, I look at Adrian's eyes, such merriment in them, with his knowing that he has asked a clever question. One that gets me thinking, and might even have caught me speechless, which his nine-year-old, competitive self would love. I say to him, "Well, this is a relationship we are creating. Like none other. Made up of you and me. So totally unique.

It isn't one that has already been mapped," and I grab his cheek as I remind him, "although I am definitely the one in charge."

I take a breath and then continue, "You and I are on a spiritual journey—up in the sky, drawing on the universe's kind energy. Our connection has been spiritual from the beginning." I tell him as I have many times before, "I meditated on your third-grade school picture for a year before you finally came, hoping that I might somehow be able to pull you into my orbit. So, we don't need a compass for work that is in the sky. Compasses are for ground work." His eyes get bigger. I somehow think he gets what I am saying. Or he has already moved on to some other galaxy of thoughts. My insides are filled with laughter. I am grinning at the way his mind works. Amazed by how closely matched we are in some ways—equally capable of asking overwhelmingly complicated philosophical questions, seemingly out of the blue.

It is a gorgeous clear winter day and all of the trees outside my study windows are sleeping. Mari—our enormously talented housemate, whom I originally met when I was studying in Cuernavaca, Mexico, and who is now in Boston on scholarship studying music—is softly strumming her guitar in the next room, getting ready to make her way to the subway to play for the day. The dogs are all at my feet, one sleeping inside the legs of my desk and two just on the other side of my desk chair. Adrian is at school, his last day before spring vacation. He took his walrus Beanie Baby, which he will play with in the car with the other Jamaica Plain car-pool children, all the way to school and probably all the way back. Such a funny combination of ages he is. Sometimes nine. Sometimes fifteen. Especially when he is tired, three, maybe two. Sometimes as vulnerable and meek as an infant.

I know some of this age-traveling is simply what nine-year-olds do, roaming around to find the tone or approach they think will get them what they want—an extra ten minutes before bed, another serving of ice cream, a story read out loud to them instead of them to you, so they won't have to hold the book. He grabs at a chance to be carried from the couch to the bed, up the many, many stairs, feigning sleep when he clearly isn't asleep, just because he wants to be carried. Somehow, I manage to get him up the stairs, feeling incredibly grateful for the two years of crew training, weight lifting, and confidence building involved in working out on a rowing machine and on the water with women coaches who know how to push women past what we think is physically and psychologically possible. I carry him up the stairs, remembering a time when I must have been about Adrian's age, although probably half his weight, pretending to be asleep so I'd get carried to bed by my second father—the man I called by his first name until my sister and I got one minute subtracted from our bedtimes each time we called him Ron instead of "Dad." I remember loving that ritual. Loving being carried by a man who seemed to easily shoulder my weight from the living room to my sister's and my bedroom, my eyes squeezed shut to make it appear I was asleep. My second father probably knew then, as I know now about Adrian, that I wasn't really asleep, but still wanted to be, needed to be, carried.

I mostly see Adrian as nine years old. Reading nine-year-old books. Playing nine-year-old games—zoom-and-make-the-Legos-fly-all-over-the-room games. But I have been struck by how often Adrian is still age-traveling with me, and I have gotten the sense that he is trying to bring all of his ages here, into this house. Wanting me to see, whether consciously or not, him at one, at three, at five, and now at nine, because I didn't get to see him then. He is doing so many things I have seen infants and very young children do — as if to find my body — to establish a history between us that time has already taken away. Six months into this journey together, he still crawls into my lap, feeling the contours of my face, my cheeks, my lips, checking how my ears attach to my face. I pull him close. He tries to root inside of me and I see how completely I can wrap my arms around him, which is no small feat given that he now weighs one hundred pounds.

In terms of intellect, he is spinning forward at lightning speed. Nine and then some. Reading forty pages at a single sitting and then running upstairs to the laptop computer his aunt Jo lent him to write a report on the book he's just finished. Nowadays he is doing all of his math homework by himself, with me still in the room but otherwise unnecessary. When he started school this year, we did all of his homework together. I sat right next to him at the kitchen table as we made it through one question at a time on his reading or math homework. I tease him now that I have become basically obsolete. He still needs my physical presence in the room when he works. He'll wander around the house with his homework in hand, following after me if I lose focus and begin watering the plants or folding laundry when he still wants me close. Now I am realizing that my main task is to ask extra questions of him after he finishes his assigned work. He loves that. Seeing if he can push himself farther than the assignments require.

So, in terms of his mind, his schoolwork, his reading, he is thriving. Absolutely thriving. The teachers at Silver Street School are helping him want to learn — letting him know, in the words of one of his teachers, that he is "wicked smart." Somehow he has risen above changing schools every year before he came to be with me. Somehow he has blocked out, or learned to discount or move beyond his stepfather's constant proclamations that Adrian was stupid. I am so relieved and grateful to see him concentrate while reading a children's science fiction novel on the couch. I beam inside when I see him *want* to do math. I laugh out loud when he comes up with several of the right questions to the *Jeopardy* answers on TV, even during the week of the *Jeopardy* championships. Last night, one of the Double Jeopardy questions asked for the name of one of the two fish that have pouches. Adrian cried out, "Seahorses!" which was right, a fact he remembered from doing a report on seahorses in third grade. I looked at him in amazement. Seahorses? Who would have thought? He has an excellent memory for numbers and facts. He scans the sports pages and remembers the scores of games and the time the Super Bowl will air weeks after he has read the information.

Meanwhile an African American parent friend of mine, whose child went through all eight years at Silver Street and is now at Harvard getting a joint Ph.D. and J.D., tells me that when her daughter was in school, she had her tested each year, independently of the school. Even though I have staunchly opposed tests to rank and segregate children, I ask my friend specifics about why and how she did that. She tells me that very few of the Black children who graduated from Silver Street last year got into competitive high schools. How can that be happening? I ask myself — the long-since-dead liberal in me momentarily rearing its head — somehow wanting to believe the playing field at Silver Street School is more level than at other schools.

But I know better than to be shocked, even to myself, as I think back two weeks, to the Martin Luther King Day assembly, where one Black child after the next got up to recite a poem, or an excerpt from one of King's speeches, but did not hold his or her head up, speak into the microphone, or bring the words on the page alive for the audience. Adrian, to my dismay, contributed to the poor performances. The night before the assembly, Adrian had sung for me the song that he and a chorus of children were going to perform at the assembly — from memory, all four verses, with no prompting whatsoever. At the assembly, however, he looked more like he was playing soccer than singing a song. During the entire song he shuffled his feet, sticking out like a very sore thumb, smack in the middle of the chorus of children, looking down, mouthing almost none of the words.

Afterward I asked him what had happened, while I tried to keep the fury out of my voice since we were in school, in a public setting. Why hadn't he given his attention to the Black woman music teacher who was directing the chorus? He told me that before the performance he had told a white teacher that he didn't know the words. She believed him, which was understandable since she probably didn't have time to question his assertion (or consider that it might have been related to his crisis of confidence, in this case, a Black crisis of confidence). So the teacher gave him the song sheet, which he put on the floor in front of him and then pushed around with his feet, no doubt trying to arrange the paper so he could see it. His chorus's "performance" had been followed by one lackluster recitation after the next, leaving my spirit wilted. Here it was. Martin Luther King Day. A high holy day in my book.

Martin Luther King Day. The holiday celebration to which Adrian had said he wanted to wear his camel hair blazer, bow tie, and white oxford-cloth, button-down shirt. I didn't know how to tell him that at Silver Street School, the children and adults would dress down for the event. I didn't yet know how to explain "dressing down" to him. How do you begin to explain the concept of "dressing down" in relation to a school where Adrian's five-year-old friend and car-pool mate brought home a caged cockroach that her class was raising as a pet? Here I am, offering to help this five-year-old carry her stuff at the end of the day when she asks me to carry the cockroach cage. I reel, having lived in (was it several?) apartments where points were definitely given to those who learned how to kill cockroaches most effectively. What does it mean for the children at Silver Street who live in apartments where landlords don't pay for pest control, who are now in a school where children are being taught to raise cockroaches for pets?

How to explain "dressing down" to Adrian when Andrea took him to Goodwill the last time she was here and bought him a maroon corduroy coat so he would have a suit coat for fancy occasions? After Andrea left, I hid the coat from Adrian—a coat that was clean and had no holes, but was definitely out of style and ill fitting. It was a marker that I didn't want marking Adrian.

I remember so well a poem written by a white, working-class single mother studying at Brandeis University—one

of the few single mothers to attend Brandeis as an under-
graduate—which included a line about buying her child
Buster Brown shoes with her welfare check. A middle-
class woman asked her why she would spend so much
money for a brand name when she should have been spending it on food. I felt that poem, remembering growing
up—much of the time—with my mother's single-parent,
high school teacher's income. I remember scurrying around
early in the morning before school, trying to find matching
clean socks for my sister and me. She and I went to a fancy,
upper-class public high school, where we had landed after
my mother's second marriage to a man from upper-middle-
class roots and where we stayed as one of the terms of the
divorce settlement. I remember deep shame rushing up into
my face, making my skin so red, with my handmade
clothes, fat body, and unmatched socks.

When Hannah offered to buy Adrian a camel hair
blazer with tailor-fitted corduroy pants so he would have
a gorgeous holiday outfit, I said, "Yes, yes, thank you, yes."
I told a friend when she offered, "I would love it if you
would get him an L.L. Bean winter coat." I am busy dressing him "up" in a school where some middle- and
upper-class parents are dressing their children "down."
Or dressing in seemingly casual wear that is actually very
expensive.

I didn't know how to explain all this to Adrian when
he asked to wear his camel hair coat, worrying, accurately
it turned out, that he would be one of the only children
wearing a suit coat for Martin Luther King's birthday. So,
without providing an accurate, or even initial political
analysis—with 6:45 in the morning quickly becoming 7:00,
the time we need to be eating in order to leave for school

at 7:30—I say to Adrian, "Let's compromise. You can wear one of the ironed button-down shirts that looks fancy." And, I reason with him, "The shirt is forest green for rich life, which is what Martin Luther King had." He looks up at me, clearly aware he is compromising, but willing to do so.

Martin Luther King Day and an assembly at a school that is trying, really trying, to get it right in terms of race. But the Black children were somehow not getting the message about projecting their voices, about standing with their chins up and eyes focused, about the drama of King's words. Neither were the white children particularly. But it is not the same. King's birthday is everybody's holiday, but especially Black people's holiday. In another place and time, before desegregation, when the Black church was the absolute center of Black community life, few Black children, by the time they were eight or nine years old, would have missed the lesson about standing tall, projecting with deep voices—giving the note, the song, the cadence, everything you have got. Black children learned that lesson in choir, on children's day at church, and in preparation for the Christmas Day pageant. And they watched their mothers and fathers and grandparents orate. And orate. And orate. That is not what is happening now at a school I wanted Adrian to go to partly *because* of its practice of quiet and meditation. A school that draws on silence and introspection, not on oratorical projection. A school I chose over the Catholic school in our neighborhood where all the students are Black and Latino (although all the teachers and administrators are white). So, I am part of the contradiction.

After the assembly, I got to spend a badly needed couple of hours with a parent, Delilah, who had preached a powerful sermon about justice at the Martin Luther King Day assembly. She spoke of her anger about the Black kids' performances, noting that all of the Black children in the older grades who participated were of Caribbean descent, a reality that further explained the lack of passion. "Just because they are Black," she says, "does not mean they necessarily have a cultural connection to or familiarity with King's life." She talked about how every year, every season, she has to speak up. Raise Cain. This isn't the first time she will be speaking up about how the African American children aren't showing the level of confidence they will need. They do need. This isn't the first time that she will go to the administrators and say that someone needs to stop the assembly and start the children over if they don't present themselves with passion and conviction. The conversation with Delilah has made me grateful to be getting to know her and tired when I realize all the work she has done.

This conversation may help explain why few of the African American children last year got into competitive high schools after Silver Street. A conversation that now makes me listen carefully as my friend tells me that she tested her daughter separately every year. That she did extra homework with her daughter on a regular basis. Adrian, it turns out, is a smart African American boy who is learning at school that he is smart. The school is pushing him forward while it may be pulling him back. In which ways, in which directions, I don't fully know yet.

For the moment, he is thriving intellectually. Running rings around *Jeopardy* questions, his math homework, and the book reports on novels he is choosing himself. Intellectually, he is clearly nine and then some. Where I see him as younger, much younger, is when it comes to his body. This child, who still doesn't know how to tie his shoes, but who asks to wear his suit coat and says he would like to wear a cape on some days— "even if the other kids don't wear capes, I don't have to follow the crowd when it comes to fashion."

When he came, he had no clue about when to stop eating. He would eat and eat and eat until I realized he had been using food to numb himself, probably for years. It took me a few weeks to realize that I needed to make it my task to serve him his food, to teach him the concept of portions. To help him find the internal gauge for "full" and "enough." This child, who throws himself into me from behind and almost knocks me over, again and again, until I finally get mad and tell him that he could puncture my kidneys if he crashes into me from behind once more. That yes, he is strong enough to really hurt the dogs as he practices riding them.

Some of this incongruity is because he is growing so fast he can't yet keep track of his height and weight. But some of it goes much deeper than his growing this year. This is much older pain. When he crawls into my arms or under my overcoat at the post office when we are standing in line, or hangs on me when we walk until I put my arm around him, I feel as if he is asking me to help him put the pieces back together. To help him connect his arms to his legs to his stomach to his head.

When I look at him, I see this incredibly handsome, broad-shouldered kid who is, in many ways, in pieces in his body. Not in pieces the way he would be had he been sexually abused. He is not afraid of any part of his body. He doesn't hold his eyes averted and away like many children who have been sexually abused. He isn't afraid to be affectionate, yet he doesn't indiscriminately show affection to everyone either. His body is intact sexually. Thankfully. Ever so thankfully. And he does not cower anymore around my unexpected touch, as he did when he first came — bracing, afraid I was going to beat him in the bathtub, bracing, afraid I was going to hit him in the face when I got mad at him. In six short months, he already seems to know that I will not beat him, take out a belt, premeditate a whipping.

But his body is still in pieces, in an early stage of integration. Fragmentation made worse because he had little chance to play sports until this year. He did not know the rules to baseball, football, hockey, basketball — all sports children play at his school — so now he is busy running to catch up, to catch on. He runs up and down the basketball court, too aggressive, so awkward, trying so hard, trying too hard, wanting to make up for lost time. In time. On time. Nine-year-old, three-year-old, having-lived-too-many-years-for-his-young-age time.

In the gaze, in the tone of the voice

PART OF WHAT I AM SEEKING is a livable space between
taking on African American culture as if it were my own
and not naming the way it has so changed me. Is it possible
for a white woman to say that she is deeply indebted to
African American culture (with the understanding that there
is no single Black culture) — as shown partly by how she
is raising her son — without making it sound like some kind
of commodity that can be tried on and worn like a piece
of clothing? It feels taboo to even raise these questions. Yet,
the five years of living with Ella and being in constant touch
with her African American family, the years I have been
teaching African American studies and learning from
African American scholars and activists, and now seeing
race through my own as well as Andrea's and Adrian's eyes
have made me a different mother than I would have been
otherwise. Still white, clearly, but also aware that there are
some white, and probably some owning-class, ways of
doing things that I don't want to reproduce. I don't want to
appropriate African American culture or take for granted
the lessons I have learned from African American life.

To think through the politics of being a parent in a
bicultural family, I find myself looking for parallels of

respectful examples of cultural fusion. I think, for instance, that I would feel respect for a Christian-raised parent who, upon losing her Jewish partner to divorce or death, might try to raise her child conscious of Jewish life and traditions. It would please me that the parent knew that a connection to Jewish culture and politics would do her son or daughter good. And I would be pleased to know that she might seek out Jews in her life to help her raise her child. In a parallel way, I am incorporating some African American values into the way I am parenting. And yet this feels scary to admit, for fear that my words will be interpreted as a sign of appropriation.

I know white parents raising children of color who are eager to expose them to African American or Latino or Native American culture—to the music, the art, the leaders, the history. That is vital, but I don't think it's enough. I am trying to go another step, to talk about a daily socialization that draws on African American ideas about child rearing. How can white parents scrutinize white parenting norms (not that there is one monolithic white way of parenting) and incorporate hard-won African American ways of doing things into everyday life?

Much of what I see many white parents permit—especially what they allow in public settings—just doesn't make sense to me. So far, I have felt I can skip a whole bunch of steps when I talk with Black or South Asian parent friends about discipline and authority that I cannot skip with most white parents. When I pick up Adrian at school, I see many interactions as parents help their children find their mittens (often lost), gather up their assignments (often still buried in their desks), and say goodbye to their classmates. In the halls, which are typically charged with energy—the kids excited about being done, the parents often hurrying, double-parked, wanting to make it out of the building with their children and all their things in a timely fashion — I see and feel a lot, including many examples of white children speaking in what I consider outrageously rude and disrespectful tones to their parents. "Mommy, get me my backpack," shouts the eight-year-old white child to her white mother. No "please." No "thank you." No eye contact. Or a ten-year-old white boy to his mother, "I am not going now. Wait in the car for me." An Asian American child who knows me well, who, even upon being reminded, sometimes does not say hello to me. Or, a bi-racial Black adopted seven-year-old girl I met at a track and field camp who, upon learning from her white mother that it was time to go home, looked straight into her mother's face and said, "I hate you. I hate you." The white mother just looked over to me, shrugged her shoulders, and said, "Oh, this happens all the time." I looked down quickly, words lost to me in that moment, although I have thought of that scene again and again since.

What does it mean for a mother, in a sexist society, to let her daughter learn to talk to adult women that way? What does it mean that a white mother lets her Black daughter think the child is in charge? Generations of media images of passive, disclaiming-their-power white women flash through my mind and I want to shake this woman. I want to say: "Don't let your daughter speak to you this way." I want to ask: "Where did you get the idea that your child being in charge would be good for her or you? Are you afraid that claiming your authority will cast you as a racist white woman (with images hearkening back to white women slaveholders)? Would you be this permissive if this child were white?" My questions to this woman overwhelm me. I walk away, nothing spoken between us, as I am aware that simply being around her threatens me.

Adrian is not immune from speaking to me rudely. But he didn't come to me with disrespectful behavior. Raised by a Caribbean-born mother and grandmother and his often-exacting big sister, Adrian learned way before me what he could and could not get away with in public and around his elders. Now, he is learning — from the media and to some extent from a multiracial, but still white-dominated, owning-class school — to be rude and arrogant by watching other children get away with it. For years I have heard Ella talk about how all her mother had to do was look at her and her sister a certain way and they knew that they had better do exactly as they were told in public. I have read many novels, poems, and historical accounts that explain how African Americans required a standard of conduct from their children in public that took into account how white people could, and often did, go off on African American children for the slightest reason. These lessons make me know that under no circumstances will I allow Adrian to get the idea that he can treat me disrespect-fully. At home or at school. Especially at school or any other public place.

Dynamics between adults and children — and the ways that class and race influence these dynamics — have led me to think carefully about where Adrian and I go together, for special events as well as for everyday outings. As much as possible, I want him to see parents and children, and grandparents and grandchildren, modeling respectful and measured relationships where the children are definitely *not* in charge. This has meant avoiding Toys R Us and

Chuck E Cheese entirely—both overstimulating scenes where children, regardless of race or class, somehow get the upper hand with their parents and then run with it. It has meant trying to dodge play dates with children whose parents let them take over the house, build forts in the living room with expensive furniture, and decide for themselves what they will eat and when they will sleep.

I have even found myself thinking carefully about where Adrian and I should go for our weekly trips to the supermarket. Supermarkets are definitely classed and raced. Over the years, I have frequented a tremendous variety of them—in the spectacularly racially mixed neighborhood of Uptown on the north side of Chicago; in a lily-white, middle-class neighborhood in Colorado Springs, where I first went to college; in the health-food capital of the world, Santa Cruz, California, where I finished college; in New Jersey; and now in Boston. The year that I lived in New Jersey in the early 1990s, the year that I met and became lovers with Ella, she and I shopped at a very upper-class independently owned grocery store. There we would shake our heads in amazement when Waspy women would reach right over Ella and grab a lemon or a cantaloupe that she had already chosen. More than once. Enough times that we learned to cross our eyes at each other and mimic the behavior, play-fighting over which one of us was going to get the lemon we had intentionally put our hands on at the same time.

Then there was the Piggly Wiggly supermarket in a mixed-class, mixed-race neighborhood in downtown Memphis, where Ella and I lived briefly in the early 1990s. Having just arrived in Memphis two days earlier, Ella and I went to the supermarket close to our house, only to be stopped, stunned, as we watched a stout African American woman with open, broken sandals and a yellowed white uniform pushing a filled-to-the-brim cart down the aisle. She walked slowly, three carefully measured and unspoken feet behind an older white ghost of a woman in peculiar clothing, whose glory had certainly seen better days. The white woman pointed and gestured all the way down the aisle, speaking in an unnecessarily loud voice to the woman, who was clearly the domestic, about exactly which brand should be put into the cart. Memphis, the same city where Ella, after pulling up to the dry cleaner in her shiny, new Volvo, was greeted by the clerk with the question, "How would she like them pressed?" As if the clothes were mine, not Ella's, although all of them — silk shirts and pants — were hers.

After the experience at the Piggly Wiggly, Ella announced we were never again going to that grocery store. She would rather drive to the other side of town. To a grocery store in a richer part of town. And we did. Often. To an independent store named Squash Blossom, the Southern version of Bread and Circus, the upscale chain of health-food markets in the Boston area. Although African American women were still doing the shopping for their white women employers, at least they were permitted to go unattended. In that upper-middle-class neighborhood, if a white woman went shopping with an African American woman, the white woman would be conveying that she wasn't wealthy enough to get "help" she could trust. At this grocery store, the food was of better quality, and not necessarily more expensive than at the one in the mixed-race, mixed-class neighborhood where Ella and I lived.

And somehow it was less painful for us to go to that store than the one close to home.

At Squash Blossom, we still witnessed white children ordering the Black women around as they pushed the children down the aisles. Ella and I still got caught in the stares of people trying to make sense of us, pushing the cart together, bantering back and forth about which brand to buy. "But Ella, Bounty is so expensive we might as well buy cloth," I would argue, the Mormon in me screeching that any paper towels, especially Bounty, were unnecessary if you had clean rags at home. She back to me, "It's Bounty or nothing. It is the only one that works." Ella, determined to teach me a sense of the extravagant, even in the kind of paper towels we bought. Me, drawn to her way of luxuriating in fancy foods and the best of kitchen supplies, still haunted by the Mormon ethic to waste nothing—not even paper towels. At Squash Blossom, Ella was still asked by seemingly kind-faced white women how she cooked collard greens. "Yours must be so good," they would say, assuming first that Ella cooked collard greens, and then that she, by virtue of being African American, carried recipes around in her head. Ella got that nonsense at Squash Blossom, but never again did we witness a white woman ordering an African American woman down each and every aisle.

How profoundly raced and classed supermarkets are has led me to think carefully about where Adrian and I shop. In Cambridge and Brookline, the Bread and Circus health-food supermarkets have their share of lemon-snatching women. In these stores, many of the clerks are South Asian or Latino and almost all of the shoppers are white and thin and dressed in 100 percent cotton. In

Jamaica Plain, for many years before the big chains were willing to invest in the neighborhood, there was Flanagans, an Irish-owned independent small supermarket that, while overpriced and well known for its soggy three-day-old produce, managed to serve a delightfully mixed-generation, mixed-ethnicity, mixed-race crowd. I always respected Flanagans for staying in Jamaica Plain during the years when no national chain would commit to the neighborhood. What ultimately drove Flanagans out was not the multicolored shoppers, but the construction of a Super Stop and Shop next to the biggest public housing building in Jamaica Plain, about a half mile from where Adrian and I live. That is where we go. Because it is close. Because it stocks Indian pickle and Bustello coffee and fresh dandelion leaves and organic milk (which is twice the price of regular milk, but I buy it anyway, haunted by the possible connection between synthetic hormones in milk products and the epidemic of breast cancer in women, especially lesbians). And, not least of all, because the children there know how to act.

At expensive supermarkets over the years, I have seen children — almost always white — constantly asking their parents: Can I have this soda? Can I have that candy? Can I have this toy? Whiny, insistent, unrelenting. My immediate, fierce reaction may have as much to do with class as with race. Growing up, I would walk alongside my mother, up and down each aisle. I would add up the total as she put each item into the basket. When clutching her list, I understood that she had carefully accounted for what she was going to buy. I guess we approximated the total, because I remember plenty of times we had to put some things back, or leave things at the register, when she didn't have enough money. So children who whine and beg for treats really grate on my nerves. When parents indulge that behavior, it seems that they are helping to create little consumers out of their children—the grocery-store version of Toys R Us, which, as National Public Radio reported, has created a horrendous new marketing strategy of creating "registries" for individual families. At Toys R Us, children can shoot an electronic gun at any toy so that relatives and friends can find and purchase exactly what little Tommy wants. This consumer culture scares me. Its connection to raising indulged and spoiled children scares me even more.

My hope to raise Adrian to be well mannered is one reason I find myself drawn to many African American modes of parenting. The tradition among many African Americans of keeping their children on a tight rein in public and teaching their children to be disciplined in stores makes sense to me. African American parents have had to keep their children close to them in public—to keep white people from putting their hands all over little Black girls' hair, to protect against white store clerks who assume that Black children, especially Black boys, intend to steal from the store. While the origins of African American parents' protectiveness are rooted in a defense against racism, the consequences include teaching Black children that they must listen to their parents in public. This reality is one reason I feel right shopping at the Super Stop and Shop in Jamaica Plain, where almost everyone is Black or Latino. At this store, Adrian sees parents and big brothers and grandmothers, often with just their eyes and sometimes with a firm tone, make it clear that whining for a treat simply won't do. He sees that the children's job is to help their parents. It is not about being entertained. He understands that shopping and paying for food can be stressful, and rarely is there enough money for everything. So best to be quiet and well mannered, the children quickly learn.

I simply don't believe in democratic parenting — in the notion that parents and children have an equal say, equal votes, an equal right to sit up in the front seat of the car, an equal right to decide on bedtime, an equal say about which music will be on the car radio, an equal right to fill the grocery basket. Maybe, by the time Adrian is sixteen or seventeen years old, some decisions can become more equal, but I think the practice that Andrea O'Reilly refers to as "sensitive mothering" can be disastrous, especially for young children. In her gutsy essay, "Ain't That Love? Antiracism and Racial Constructions of Motherhood," O'Reilly writes that white middle-class expectations for mothering in the 1990s — what is considered "good mothering" — is "child centered." This mothering is characterized by "flexibility, spontaneity, democracy, nurturance, and playfulness." A mother's day is supposed to revolve around her children — not her housework as in the 1950s, but around her children's educational development.[1] Key to this development is the notion that children should be seen and heard, at all times, whether they know what they are talking about or not, whether they are interrupting adults or not, whether they have been listening to the conversation or not. According to O'Reilly, and I agree, this model of parenting assumes that leisure time exists and that a culture is anxiously awaiting a child's every contribution.

For Adrian, neither exists. Neither of us has much leisure time between school and work demands. And he

certainly is not growing up in a culture that will easily
embrace him — the smart, clearheaded, and sensitive
African American boy that he is and the man he will
hopefully become. O'Reilly writes, "In working class
households, the boundaries between mothering and domestic labor are maintained and the very real work of domestic
labor is not transformed — not trivialized — into a game
for the child's benefit."[2] Hence my *un*willingness to try to
make shopping fun.

For me, as a single mother from a mixed-class background who is now trying to hang on to middle-class status
while supporting three people — Andrea, Adrian, and
me — abdicating my power would make little sense. I am
already aware that Adrian responds to my requests more
quickly when I speak in a low register, rather than my
natural first-soprano voice. My friend Delilah told me that
she deliberately lowers her voice when she means business
with her twelve-year-old son. He and Adrian have already
come to believe that lower — i.e., male — voices carry more
authority than higher voices. Adrian is surrounded — in
cartoons, in the newspaper, in sitcoms, in the movies —
with images of ineffectual white women, always second to
their men. There is a dearth of images of white women
who confront racism in schools, in the courts, or at the
neighborhood police department.

I want Adrian to know that I am in charge, that I mean
what I say, and that he can trust my words and actions.
I want him to know, in his bones, that I am capable of
taking him on — inside and outside the house — if need
be. It is important to me that he knows I can do 250 sit-
ups without stopping. That I can run six miles before
breakfast and still playfully pick him up and toss him across

the room. I know that eventually the situation will be physically reversed. At 105 pounds, he can already pick me up high and hold me there. But by the time he can outwrestle, outrun, outsprint, and outbench-press me, I hope that my moral authority will be absolutely secure. I want him to know that I want to hear his perspective and that I care about how he sees the world. But, by virtue of my age, experience, and love for him, what I have to say counts. A child-rearing ethic where women are clearly in charge is not white-inspired. Some white families draw a distinct line of authority between parent and child. But I have seen more regard within African American families for adults because of their age and experience, and a willingness among parents to provide strict limits to what children can do and say.

Last night, Adrian and I ate dinner at the home of Issac and Charlotte Berman. Because of their age and emerging relationship to Adrian, they are becoming significant elders in his community. Issac, with his deep, resonant, and wise voice, was reading from a biography of Malcolm X, a book Adrian is also reading as background material for an upcoming school presentation. During the reading, Adrian interrupted Issac several times to ask if we could stop and play Monopoly instead. At first, I tried to let Adrian know with my eyes that he needed to stop his foolishness. When that didn't work, I had to ask Issac to stop reading for a moment to let Adrian know that his only acceptable move was to sit and listen attentively until it was his turn to read again. During the car ride home, I explained—or, more accurately, preached—why it was totally unacceptable to not listen intently when a man in his seventies was offering a powerful rendering of Malcolm X's writing.

When Adrian had slipped out of the room during our visit, I had turned to Issac and explained that it was important that I not back down, that we teach Adrian to listen quietly, that games were a lowest common denominator that we didn't have to succumb to every time we got together. Issac said that he had always been a pushover. "I always gave in when I was raising my kids," he told me, "but I guess they turned out all right." I agreed. They had. His two now-grown children are sensitive, interested in the world, and socially conscious. Issac has spent his life learning—with much help from his feminist wife and lesbian daughter—that being a white man does not mean having to run over and through people. In fact, his humanity has been based on doing quite the opposite— adopting a power-with, rather than a power-over, way of being in the world. In the 1940s, Issac was kicked out of the Communist Party because he questioned its authoritarian, doctrinaire structure. Issac, the man who cofounded the cocounseling movement—a self-help, peer-counseling method that challenged Freudian and top-down brands of therapy. This man, whose willingness to share power with me when I was a beginning graduate student at Brandeis University in the 1980s—by asking me to be his teaching assistant and then letting me take on many responsibilities—is the reason I believed I might be able to make it through my first years in a doctoral program.

Looking into Issac's kind, sweet eyes, I tried to explain that his situation as a parent wasn't the same as mine is now. Class and gender divide our situations. His abdication of his power as a white man raising children in a heterosexual, middle-class family was not the same as what I am trying to do. Adrian was *not* going to get a sense of the need to respect his elders from the white culture around him—where older people are often thrown away, sent to nursing homes, and set up for earlier and earlier retirements. Adrian was going to need to learn how to respect elders here, in the Bermans' house. Adrian was going to need to know manners that white children would not be held accountable for. Adrian cannot afford to go through childhood without learning about diction, about reading out loud with intensity, about performing with the written word. In this multiracial community that is helping to raise him, it is up to us to teach him. In this instance, Issac, Charlotte, and me—two Jews, and a Mormon so changed by the civil rights, gay and lesbian, and feminist movements—these adults, are the ones in charge. Adrian needs that. So do I.

Much of the script, already written

ADRIAN IS IN THE LAST STAGES of preparing his oral presentation at Silver Street on Malcolm X's life. In the fall, we had read a book together on Malcolm X and Adrian had read another, more advanced book at school during the winter. So, when it came time for the children to decide which famous person to focus on for their six-week project, Adrian chose Malcolm X. I was glad that the teachers knew enough about Malcolm to put him on the list of possible choices. And I was happy that Adrian chose him of his own volition — that he would have a chance to do enough reading to go beyond the stereotype, beyond the one-dimensional caricatures of Malcolm reflected in consumer representations of his life — in the Malcolm X baseball caps and T-shirts.

Angela Davis has cautioned against such caricatures. Over the years, she has been remembered more for her Afro hairstyle in the 1960s than for the politics and accomplishments of Black activists of that era. Davis writes in "Afro Images: Politics, Fashion and Nostalgia,"

It is both humiliating and humbling to discover that in a generation following the events that constructed

*me as a public personality, I am remembered as a
hairdo. It is humiliating because it reduces a politic of
liberation to a politic of fashion, it is humbling because
such encounters with the younger generation demon-
strate the fragility and mutability of historical images,
particularly those associated with African American
history.*[1]

Karl Marx, too, has taken a hit of late, with his image
now used to advertise popular bars and dance parlors in
New York City and Paris. He might, if he believed in a
spirit beyond death, turn over in his grave to know that
his image is helping to further, even advertise, an accumu-
lation of private profit for a beer joint. With Davis's lament
and caution and the image of Marx's fury, I was glad that
Adrian was going to have the time, in elementary school,
to study Malcolm X's life in depth.

Of course, Adrian was ecstatic to learn that we would
need to find him a fancy black coat, tie, and pants to wear
for the presentation, since Malcolm always dressed to the
nines once he got out of prison and joined the Nation of
Islam. Adrian loved the idea of wearing a dinner jacket
since, from the time he first came to live with me, he had
asked for a tuxedo — a sign, I am hoping, that he will be a
natty dresser when he grows up. So Hannah found Adrian
a dinner jacket and fancy tuxedo pants in the costume room
of a community theater and brought them home for him
to try on. He paraded around the house looking tall and
gorgeous as he added, in his words, "the finishing touches"
by putting on, over the coat, a bright red cape that he
had adorned himself with many times in the past. Usually
Adrian had worn this cape as it was designed, to go on

top of a red leotard with jewels at the neck and on the sleeves. This time, with the red cape on top of the dinner jacket and pants and a skinny bow tie, he began to practice the excerpt he had chosen from one of Malcolm X's speeches.

When I had first bought him a copy of Malcolm X's speeches, I directed him to the one Malcolm had delivered to Mississippi Youth in 1964 because I thought that Malcolm X's audience that day—young activists in the South—might resonate with the nine- and ten-year-olds in Adrian's class. But since nothing in that speech grabbed Adrian, I suggested that he choose two to three paragraphs from some other speech that would work for his presentation. I left him with the book of speeches as I ran into Home Depot to get a light for Andrea's room—one of the seemingly countless projects I have been trying to do around the edges to keep our hundred-year-old house standing and lit. When I came out of the store with the light and pansies in tow (on a gorgeous spring day who can resist a flat of pansies to plant with a child who has been begging for a garden?), Adrian looked brightly in my direction and announced that he had chosen the passage from "The Black Revolution." Adrian read to me as I was driving home:

> So today, when the Black man starts reaching out for what America says are his rights, the Black man feels that he is within his rights . . . to do whatever is necessary to protect himself. An example of this was taking place last night at this same time in Cleveland, where the police were putting water hoses on our people there and also throwing tear gas at them — and they

met a hail of stones, a hail of rocks, a hail of bricks. A couple of weeks ago in Jacksonville, Florida, a young teen-age Negro was throwing Molotov cocktails.

Well, Negroes didn't do this ten years ago. But what you should learn from this is that they are waking up. It was stones yesterday, Molotov cocktails today; it will be hand grenades tomorrow and whatever else is available the next day. The seriousness of this situation must be faced up to. You should not feel that I am inciting someone to violence. I'm only warning of a powder-keg situation. You can take it or leave it. If you take the warning, perhaps you can still save yourself. But if you ignore it or ridicule it, well death is already at your doorstep. There are 22 million African-Americans who are ready to fight for independence right here. When I say fight for independence right here, I don't mean any non-violent fight, or turn-the-other-cheek fight. Those days are gone. Those days are over.[2]

After Adrian read the passage, I commended him for choosing a "by any means necessary" passage, since that goes to the heart of Malcolm's politics for most of his life. As Adrian began to read it out loud in the car — that would be the only moment that day before bedtime when he could practice with me as his audience — he made it through the difficult passage and only tripped over what, to me, were fairly esoteric phrases. He asked me to explain what a Molotov cocktail was. "That is a homemade bomb, Adrian," I told him. "What is a hand grenade?" he asked me. "That is a bomb that a person throws by hand that is a lot like the land mines you protested in the letter your class wrote to President Clinton last fall," I explained.

I explained the terms and praised him for reading it so well out loud for the first time. Then he read it again, and again, each time getting closer to a cadence of speech he remembered from Denzel Washington's rendition of Malcolm X in Spike Lee's film on Malcolm X's life. Adrian especially liked the line, "If you take the warning, perhaps you can still save yourself"—a warning that it was up to white people to take racism seriously. He also thought that the kids might like the passage's reference to hand grenades, since discussions of explosions and rockets seem to be daily bread in nine-year-old boys' conversations.

As the day of his performance got closer, Adrian's attitude toward the passage began to change. I first noticed this when he couldn't remember to bring Malcolm X's speeches home from school so we could practice. He began to tell me that he wasn't going to read from Malcolm X's speeches at all. He was, though, willing to talk about the aspects of Malcolm X's life that he thought were the most important. Each point he emphasized seemed to resonate with struggles Adrian had already lived through. Adrian explained to me, "When Malcolm X's father died—or maybe was killed by white people—Malcolm didn't know who he could count on and everything seemed out of control." "That's like me," he added, in an understated way, having never known his father or grandfather and having been often separated from his biological mother. Adrian continued, "Malcolm's mother went a little bit crazy after her husband's death and then the authorities took the children from their mother and put them in separate homes."

Adrian and his two younger siblings knew about foster care from personal experience.

Adrian explained to me, "Malcolm was called 'home boy' in Harlem in reference to his good dancing and having come from the country." When I asked Adrian why that detail was important to him, he explained that he had been called "country boy" last summer, at an urban camp where the children were unfamiliar with African American children who had not grown up in Boston. I told Adrian that "home boy" is considered a sign of affection, which is different from what the kids meant by "country boy." "But it is true," I told him, "that both you and Malcolm X spent some time growing up in the country." Adrian continued his story of Malcolm's life: "When Malcolm met Betty, he began to feel safe and believe in himself. That's what I am doing now, learning to feel safe."

As Adrian continued to account for the story of Malcolm X's life, I was amazed by how much of what he focused on was about relationships and families. He was keying in on Malcolm X's life on so many levels. He told me about how Malcolm X wore his hair. "The conking burned his scalp terribly," Adrian said, informing me that he could have avoided that entirely by growing an Afro. He explained why Malcolm X tried to find his sister in Boston, a subtheme in Malcolm's life that parallels Adrian's deep love for his older sister. Adrian said that Malcolm X gave up cigarettes in prison because, "like you, Malcolm believed that the body is a temple."

Adrian told me that, based on the books he has read, he thinks that meeting Betty Shabazz turned Malcolm's life around the most. When I asked him why he saw that as the point of greatest transition, Adrian said: "Big love

can be all powerful." He continued, "Malcolm knew psy-
chically and emotionally that his life was in danger on a
daily basis." No words were spoken between us on this
point, just a long-held gaze, with the shared knowing of
the many times Adrian's own life had been in danger. He
ended his rendering with, "What Malcolm taught me was
to stand up for myself and believe in my dreams." Okay,
kid, run with that lesson, I thought to myself. Something
mighty powerful in Adrian has always helped him move
forward. By this point in Adrian's rendition, I was smiling
to the point of bursting, marveling at the strength of his
spirit, which continues to protect him.

As Adrian's essay on Malcolm X's life grew and his
capacity to remember specific details made his speech
longer and longer, he continued to "forget" the book of
Malcolm X's speeches at school, which meant it was impossible for us to practice his presentation. When I finally
asked him if there was something about the speech itself
that made it hard for him to remember to bring the book
home, he said he just couldn't say the speech he had chosen.
That night, long after he had first fallen asleep, Adrian
came stumbling into my bedroom with tears in his eyes,
telling me he had been having a dream where some people
were throwing hand grenades at him. He told me through
the tears, "I am not going to read that speech in class. It is
scaring me. We have to look for another speech." I agreed.
No speech is worth having a nightmare about. He told me
about how, in the dream, hand grenades were being thrown
at him. From what he had told me before, this dream
seemed to be the third in a trilogy of dreams about damage done to him, danger he has faced, and ways he has
moved away from it.

In the first dream (which he had in the fall), his step-father, Damion, had flown a fighter plane from Idaho to Boston in order to drop a bomb on our house. In the dream, Adrian and I had miraculously gotten safely out of the house with the dogs. We had gone up the street to ask men working on a construction site if they could help us rebuild our house. The upside of the dream, as I saw it, was that we had made it out safely and together. And he saw me as someone who could find help in order to get the house fixed. The downside was that he felt so vulnerable to Damion's violence. It was amazing to see how immediately his face relaxed — and how literal the dream had been to him — once I told him that Damion couldn't fly a fighter plane from Idaho to Boston, since the authorities would not permit him to leave the airport.

In the second of the three dreams, Adrian flew a plane through our three-story house, dropping flowers on each floor of the house. When he first told me that dream, I felt such a calm about me as this child, at least in his dreams, saw himself as bringing goodness and beauty into the house. When he told me about the third dream — where people were throwing hand grenades at him — I asked him who was doing the damage, but he didn't know. In his dream, it didn't so much matter *who* was throwing the grenades as that they were aimed in his direction.

With this dream, told to me amidst racking sobs, the most I knew to do was to ask Adrian to close his eyes and imagine a clear bulletproof bubble surrounding him. I told him that he could see out of the bubble but no one could see into it unless he wanted them to. I told him he could visualize that bubble to protect himself if the dream ever happened again. Or, we would visualize it together. He seemed to like the idea of a protective bubble. We visualized it together until he told me that he got it — that he could clearly see it with his eyes closed. I sat with him, our eyes still closed, so thankful for the years of spiritual work that have helped me use visualization in the face of powerlessness. Even if that visualization cannot protect him from an actual bullet, it may at least protect him from attacks taking place in his mind. Dreams of attacks, so likely fueled by years that Damion abused Adrian, of Damion hitting him from behind and when Adrian was naked, of Damion getting drunk at night and then driving with the family — Grace, Andrea, Adrian, Josie, and Adam — in a car, huddled together, fearing for their lives. Attacks now remembered through a speech by Malcolm X that I had naively thought would somehow bolster Adrian.

We began to look for a new excerpt from Malcolm X's speeches — perhaps a speech after Malcolm had come back from Mecca, at the point in his life when he still believed in self-determination and self-defense, but no longer linked an antiracist politic with a separatist one. As we searched, I thought about how utterly complicated it must have been for Adrian to make sense out of the first excerpt. In the speech, the hand grenades were thrown by the Black men in self-defense when the white police officers met the protesters with guns and tear gas. In his dream, Adrian became the target, perhaps as the Black boy assaulted by a white man, his stepfather, all his life. As the target of his stepfather's abuse, Adrian had already suffered the damage and he was just now getting a chance to start to heal from it. Last week I heard him say to a friend that Damion "didn't deserve to be my father. He doesn't know how to treat children right." Inside, I smiled a big, thankful smile, hearing him say words I had said to him in various versions: "Adrian, 'father' is a term people need to earn. It is a term of respect that Damion is not worthy of."

A second possible target he could have been dreaming about — as an African American boy now being raised by a white mother — might not have occurred to me had I not recently interviewed an antiracist working-class white activist who has raised a biracial son. She spoke with clarity about how her now-grown son told her that he was sometimes afraid for her, protective of her, when he was growing up. In the Black neighborhood where they lived when he was a young boy, he had sometimes worried that she might be targeted — a concern she had never shared, partly because she knew the neighborhood well. Her son also remembers not telling her about scapegoating and hostility he faced at school. He had not wanted to worry her and was not sure she could do anything about it. Sometimes, because he felt to blame somehow for the scapegoating, he chose not to involve her. During our conversation, this woman told me, "Black kids try to protect white parents in all kinds of ways, big and small, rarely named." This was a truly scary thought to me, when my number one job is to try to protect Adrian. This may be why, in Adrian's dream, the grenades that Malcolm X said Black men were throwing at white authorities were now aimed at Adrian — this time by unknown people.

Adrian recently told a friend of mine that if anyone ever tried to bother him, he knew that I "would jump down from a big tower and bang up the bad guys and scoop me up and away." Perhaps, in some version of his story of how he came to live with me, he sees me as having done that—of having sent an airplane ticket to him in Idaho so that he could come, stay, and eventually live with me. Maybe, hopefully, he carries that image of me around with him. But in the day-to-day, much is left unsaid, since he has little language for what he is experiencing in terms of race and class. Even if he did have the words, he might be too tired to talk it out with me anyway.

Meanwhile, nine months into what I hope will be our life together, Adrian and I will find another excerpt from one of Malcolm X's speeches, so that we can work together on diction and eye contact with the audience, projecting his voice, emphasizing the verbs, so that the audience can visualize what he is describing. We will go through the new excerpt again and again. I will show him James Earl Jones's magnificent performance of his one-man play about Paul Robeson's life, while I teach him visualizations I learned from meditation to counter nightmares. I recite to myself the words from Kahlil Gibran's poem, "On Children":

> *Your children are not your children.*
> *They are the sons and daughters of Life's longing for*
> *   itself.*
> *They come through you but not from you*
> *And though they are with you,*
> *Yet they belong not to you.*

A song to remind me that Adrian has his own spiritual guide, his own power animal—which, he informs me, is indeed powerful. The truth is that no matter how much I try to protect him, advise him, listen to him, much of the script of his life is already written. He is already a survivor, having found a way (with the help of his mother, sister, and me) to be freed of his stepfather's abuse. He has already beaten the odds as he remains engaged and interested in school at an age when many teachers start to give up on Black children, boys in particular. I will, in my meditations, say quiet prayers that some bubble will follow him in his life — protecting his head and body from hand grenades aimed in his direction. I pray that I will listen to him carefully and understand injuries he will face that my white socialization has taught me not to see or confront. I pray that I can remain the adult, the parent, in a society where African American children are asked, required, to be white people's protectors and witnesses, from very young.

Father love

I'T'S NINE IN THE MORNING and I am already weary
from the day, wondering whether there is any stand I can
take that would represent a place of justice. I don't think
so. Life feels vexed from every direction.

After driving Adrian and his six-year-old friend to
school this morning, listening to them make up stories
about Beanie Babies that could catapult into other realities, I noticed a person on the side of the road stooped
over. At first I could barely make out whether the person
was a man or a woman. The sun streaming into my window forced me to squint to even see a figure. But the steady
stoop and the plastic bags all around the figure made me
turn my car around, worried that someone might have
fallen. As I got closer, I saw the shape was a man, a
homeless man, who was trying to gather up his filled-to-
the-brim-with-papers plastic bags while coaxing a twig
out of a crack in the sidewalk.

I pulled over in my Honda, the ever reliable Etta
James, and looked in my wallet, hoping that I had more
than a couple of dollars left from grocery shopping the day
before. Between my wallet and the tolls compartment in
the car, I had only two dollar bills and a bunch of change.

Not much, but enough for a cup of coffee and a donut. I walked over to him to give him the money. I didn't want to startle him, since he was still bent over working on the twig, so I spoke softly: "Good morning. Sorry I don't have more. Here's a little money for some hot breakfast."

Big, warm smile from him. Such kind eyes. And a "Thank you. Happy Easter to you and your family and your friends." I thought to myself, yes, Easter and Passover. A Passover seder on Friday with Jo and her daughter and Andrea and Adrian and many of Jo's other friends. Easter on Sunday, celebrated in Brookline, with two Jewish women and their daughters. We'll go to the seder on Friday and hide the matzo for Adrian to find and then hide Easter eggs for the children to find on Sunday. I look up at the man's face, wondering if I could tell him all that. Still a smile from him. I smile back. Our eyes meet. And hold each other. And hold each other. Then I get shy, and turn toward my car. Get in, turn the car around. I look behind to see if he might still be looking up so I could wave. And he is. I wave. He waves. He waves bigger. I wave bigger. Until we are both waving wildly, he on the curb, me from my car. Sun streaming. Cool, warm, early spring day. All the way down the street. My eyes looking behind him to keep him in my sights as the car drives forward. He, still waving, from the side of the road. My waving back.

And then big, big elephant tears, streaming out of my eyes. Marveling at the connection, on this sun-filled morning, with a man I do not know. Big tears flowing, with images of my father, his spirit inside of me, the father who spent many nights (and days) on the streets — sometimes sleeping in cardboard boxes. The father who died in a one-room studio apartment outside Salt Lake City, in an apartment he liked because, since it was in the middle of the building, it drew on the warmth of the other units and so cost less to heat. The father who took homeless people in on more than one occasion. The father who told me that he had been in at least seventy jails in his lifetime. Not so much with a bragging tone, but definitely to let me know he had been around. The father whose presence I feel in such unexpected moments. Now waving at me, from the side of the road. Waving widely. Huge smile. Tears streaming, still. I see him on that street. I see him whenever I pass a man working with a jackhammer, work my father used to do for pay, on his good days, in the good months, when he wasn't drinking. The father whose gifts left to me after he died included *Alice in Wonderland,* a book of Kahlil Gibran's poetry, and a little wooden piggy bank that said, "A penny for every swear word." From the way my father talked, I guess he could have saved a lot of pennies in that bank.

Last year my grandfather told me a story about a time when I was four or five and he came over to the house by the fairgrounds in Phoenix, Arizona, where I lived with my mother and sister. It was New Year's Day and my father had been out drinking all night long. That morning, my grandfather had found him on the curb in front of our house, saying that he didn't want any help from my grandfather, that he needed to get through the hangover from the night before by himself. When I asked my grandfather if he remembered where I was at the time, he said, "Oh, you were just a baby. You wouldn't remember that. You were much too young."

My grandfather kept reminiscing, assuming he was right—that youth had protected me from the scene.

Meanwhile, my mind careened back in time, to a scene of my father on the curb. A scene that, until that moment, had been tucked away, but now rushed forward. The little girl, looking out the window of the house by the fairgrounds... Oh! I see you out the window. You came home, Daddy. There you are. Sitting on the curb in front of our house. I'll just slip out of the window since Mommy and Jasmine are still asleep. Slip out the window and surprise you. You came home. Daddy, I am coming. I am coming toward you. I'll surprise you in my slippers and Kentucky Fried Chicken T-shirt. I'll welcome you back. Mommy and Jasmine will be glad to see you. Hi, Daddy. Here I am.

Big hug to you. I have been calling you via our invisible wire. Did you get the message? Come on in, Daddy. We'll get sardines and saltines. Graham crackers and milk. Let's eat breakfast together. Then you can take us to the sitter. Mommy has to go to work. Maybe we can go to the swings after that. Won't that be fun?

Daddy, how come you aren't talking? Come on, Daddy. Get up. What do you mean you wanna stay out here, sitting on the curb? Your head hurts? You stayed out too late? The world is going to be mad at you now? You better stay out here 'til you feel better? Come on, Daddy. Come into the house. Jasmine will be awake soon. We'll get you some food.

I missed you, Daddy. We watched the bell go to the top of the tower in New York City last night on TV. Johnny Carson and lots of other people announcing. Saying it's a new year. Gong, and the lights in the city on the TV went crazy. Daddy, you would have liked it. Me and Jasmine watched, kind of from our bedroom since we were supposed to be asleep. Mommy didn't know we were awake. She fell asleep after she got home from being with you. Did you have fun? The two of you? Come on, Daddy, get up. Let's go in and surprise Jasmine and Mommy. We gotta get ready to go to the sitter. Workday, remember? What, Daddy? I can barely hear you. It's not a workday 'cause it's New Year's Day? Well, okay. Then we can go to the swings, right? I'll pull you up. Ready? No? You wanna stay out here? It'll get hot, Daddy. It's going to be sunny today. You'll be lonely out here. I don't want to go back to the house alone. I can't get back in the window without a push and the door is locked. Help me find the hidden key, Daddy. I'll show you where it is. Mommy locked the door, she said, so you couldn't get in drunk. Let's eat some treats, Daddy. Daddy, get up.

Thirty-five years later, and still the daughter of a man who was a plumber's helper and a rebel who, in his own words a few years before he died, "just liked the taste of whiskey too much." My father left me with eyes that seem to let in a lot of pain. Pain for the world. Horror at the injustices I am part of, as I am now in an economic class position that is part of the problem. I arrive home from the commute as the tears on my cheeks are drying from the warmth of the car. I pull up to the curb at my house alongside a man who is mute, who is going through each of the recycling bins looking for returnable cans. His pushcart has folded in on itself, so he is having a hard time getting it to stand up again. He finally urges it in the direction he is walking as he goes from one bin to the next, empty-handed. In this neighborhood, which sits adjacent to a poorer one, this man is late, in the scheme of things, coming in the morning when the recycling has already been sorted through by others the night before. I say good morning to him. He moves his lips, but he has no words. I look into his face as I feebly go through the recycling in hopes of finding something I can hand to him. I am, in that moment, part of the problem, about to walk into my house, where I am the owner, not the tenant, a position made possible with the down payment from a wealthy friend—with money, earned through generations that have benefited from the unearned privileges of whiteness. Tears in my eyes, tears in my eyes, as I am waiting, waiting....

A close friend of mine told me a story about a dog that lives next door to her house. The people who "own" the dog leave him outside for hours and hours at a time. He protests by whining loudly, for hours on end. Eventually my friend talked with the neighbors, asking them to care for the dog, but to no avail. Calling the authorities didn't help. My friend and her partner contemplated moving, but decided not to, which meant they were left to listen to the dog as they tried to continue on with their lives, lives that center on quiet and meditation, in a house that feels very much like an ashram. I asked her how she could do that, how she could listen to the suffering day and night. She said that over time there was a lesson to be learned. She tells me, "There are children dying all over the world, at this minute, dying of hunger, in the arms of those who love them. The universe hears their screaming and witnesses their suffering. You can't just close the suffering off. It is all around us." I am left wondering what tremendous toll it takes on adults, as well as children, as they learn to screen suffering out. And then worse, as we begin to think we are not part of the problem, we are somehow separate, not responsible, not connected with it.

Living amid class inequality is really about learning to tell lies—for the sake of propriety. This morning, Adrian and I ran into the father of one of the two boys in Adrian's class with whom I think Adrian is beginning to feel safe. This child wants Adrian to come visit his house, since they already had an "overnight" at our house. Seeing the father on the sidewalk, Adrian asked if he could come over and visit his friend. The father said to Adrian and then to me, "Yes, we would love to have you over to our house on the ocean, but we are on our way to Europe for two weeks and then away traveling for a weekend, but when we get back...let's arrange it. Would that be okay, Adrian?" Adrian looked up and said, "Oh, that will be fine. Thank you." A lie coming right out of his mouth. Easy as warm honey. A lie that he somewhere learned to tell for the sake of propriety.

Class at ear-piercing levels, made completely silent in that exchange. They off to Europe as I am worrying about how to scrape together the extra thousand dollars required for tuition next year since Adrian's financial aid package remained the same, even though my expenses have sky-rocketed. They off to Europe as I worry about tuition as the homeless man on the street works on getting the twig out of the crack in the sidewalk, as the silent man in front of the house I own goes through the recycling bin that offers him no return. Somehow, Adrian is learning to make sense out of all that, and I know little about how to help him since we are part of the problem.

Mother love

IT IS THE END OF APRIL, in the midst of springtime, and I am just now starting to grieve for the life I had before Adrian came. These first several months — August, September, October, November, December, January, February, March — have been so full and intense: enrolling Adrian in school, going to a doctor and a dentist, meeting a new family of friends, borrowing a computer, buying toys, books, a warm comforter, shoes and boots, and the list goes on. I haven't had a moment to remember any time before he came. I squint inside to try to remember if I ever *had* a life before August. What did I do with transitions? What did I do with the two hours in the morning I now spend commuting? What did I do with my hours at night when I now fall into bed, exhausted, immediately after putting him to bed? When did I get those unmistakable wrinkles around my mouth and eyes? Why do I yearn for quiet, for solitude, and then spend so many of those rare precious moments thinking about him? How did I even think I was up to this task?

Eight months into it, I am finally starting to realize how infinitely more complicated almost everything I do is now. This is nothing that other mothers, other fathers, other caretakers don't already know. But because it was such instant motherhood, such an instant change in life, I am somehow running to catch up with myself, wondering how I can possibly rise to the seemingly daily challenges I have never encountered before.

One of the most vexing issues I have been thinking about has to do with Adrian's mother, Grace. I feel myself constantly balancing on an invisible live electrical wire, feeling scorched but knowing I need to stay on the wire to walk Adrian through his emotional changes. In some ways, this changing of the guard, this laying on of new hands, this handoff from one woman to the next, is strikingly straightforward. Grace had been mothering Adam, who has had an extreme case of asthma since he was an infant, Josie, her precocious and energetic four-year-old, and Adrian, who looks and acts more like a twelve-year-old. Grace has been battered by Damion for seven years, has watched her husband blow smoke into Adam's face while the toddler was having an asthma attack, has watched Damion take the rent money and run. She has watched Damion beat Adrian over and over again. Damion routinely told Adrian he was worthless and accused him of wanting to make something of himself. Finally Grace came to a place where she decided that letting Adrian go was an act of love. With great labor and sadness, I can only surmise, she decided to hand her child over to someone she believes will give her child great love.

In "Ain't That Love," Andrea O'Reilly explains that the dominant model of mothering in this country assumes that a mother should keep her child with her at all costs, no matter what.[1] This model fails to take into account the many reasons that sending a child away can be the best choice for the child. I think of a former student of mine at the University of Massachusetts at Boston whose parents left her in the Dominican Republic with her grandmother when they moved to the United States because they feared for their lives in that country due to political repression. They decided that they could not care for their daughter and immigrate, too. I think of parents in urban areas who send children to boarding schools during the academic year and to rural areas in the summer or to school in faraway school districts to protect them from possible violence. In response to adopted children who grow up thinking their biological mothers were bad mothers, O'Reilly writes, "If [a] mother could have told her daughter that her survivalist type of mother-love — mothering as separation — *was* an expression of mothering as good as, if not better than the dominant mode, perhaps there would have been less blame and more understanding between mother and daughter."[2] I want as much understanding and as little blame as possible between Adrian and me, between Adrian and his mother, between his mother and me. It's hard to find that balance, though.

Last night, Adrian had a sleepover with two new friends, eight- and eleven-year-old brothers. After much discussion, the three kids and I decided they could sleep in the same room together as long as they actually slept. Fat chance, I knew, but Adrian had been yearning for company at night since he had always slept near his younger sister and brother before he came to be with me. I also knew that there is something about turned-off lights and being under bedcovers that can invite a special kind of intimate talk among sleepover mates.

The three boys settled in quietly with two of our three big dogs at their feet. I heard not a word until Adrian came in to tell me he was sad, very sad, because he missed his mother. I gave him a quick hug, and, as I try to do, told him that his feelings made total sense. How could he not miss her? But, I reasoned, "How about going back into the bedroom with the two boys and telling them?" He said that he was afraid they would make fun of him if they saw him crying. I said that he would never know how they would respond unless he gave them a chance. He dragged his pillow back into the other room while I remained in my bed, hoping that they would really listen to him as he told them about the longing he carries around. I was betting on them being able to come through for him since they had been seeing less of their father of late because of his abusive behavior.

No sound came from the room of the three boys. Total quiet as I wondered what to do. I couldn't go in and say, "Hey guys, how did you do? Did you care for Adrian as he cried? Adrian, did you tell them?" I couldn't really say, "I know you two can relate to his mother loss, since you two rarely see your father now." So, I lay in my own bed wondering, until Adrian came in to tell me that the eight-year-old was very upset. He was missing his mother a lot. I asked Adrian to send the eight-year-old in, which he did. I wrapped him in blankets to keep him warm and then asked him to visualize where his mother was right now — most probably sitting on her sofa as she does in the evening, reading a book, pondering how to write the dissertation she has been working on. He said that if he closed his eyes, he could see her. I asked if he could send her some love through the airwaves. We could do it together, I offered.

He looked at me quizzically, and then said, "Yes," clearly
the type, even at his young age, to try anything at least
once. We visualized together. Then he said he felt better.
He got up. Went into the other room to the warmth of his
brother on one side and Adrian on the other with the dogs
at the foot of the bed.

Maybe twenty minutes later Adrian came in again to
tell me that he was *really* missing his mother this time. The
boys had listened to him and had understood but still, he
said, he needed to sleep with me. He got into my bed and
started to talk, telling me he was really confused. "How
could she send me away? Why did she send me away?" he
asked painfully. Not new questions, but clearly worth dis-
cussing again. Then new questions from Adrian: "Why
doesn't my mommy tell me how she is really doing when
we talk on the phone each Sunday morning? Why does
she avoid the questions I ask about her and then talk about
Josie and Adam instead?" I marveled that he even noticed
that she was avoiding his questions. I was amazed that
he was asking her to say how she was doing and that he
noticed that she wasn't getting deep with him. I told him I
was impressed with his perceptiveness — that maybe on
Sunday he could ask her how she was doing and then
stick with the question until he felt certain she had really
answered it.

He seemed satisfied for the moment with that approach,
but then moved on. He said he was very confused. "How
did I get here?" he asked. I told him again, "Your mother
wanted you to be in a place where you could grow in every
direction — emotionally, intellectually, spiritually. She knew
this would be a place where that could happen." A few
days before, I had asked him what was most different

about living with me in Boston rather than living with his mother in Idaho. After some thought, he said that the buildings were the most different. At first I was totally puzzled by the answer, but then I figured it out. The actual structure is totally different in almost every way from what he was used to. A child raised Seventh-Day Adventist now living in a home where "eclectic" might be the only term to describe the spirituality I practice. A child raised mostly in poverty, now living with me as I hang on by my fingernails to middle-class status. A child raised in a heterosexual, patriarchal family now being raised by a village of people, many of whom are lesbians. The contrasts are stunning. Perhaps the only common denominator between the past and the present is that I know both Grace and I love Adrian deeply.

When I said that his mother wanted the best for him by sending him to me, Adrian conceded that was partly true. He *was* getting things educationally that he wouldn't have been able to get in Idaho. I agreed, having carried a frightening picture in my head of what it would have been like for him to continue going to public school in a rural, very small town in southern Idaho, where, according to his mother, she and the children were the only people of color. Adrian was willing to say that his educational opportunities are better in Boston, but he was unwilling to go farther—to say that he is safer than before. For him, perhaps, saying such things might make him feel as if he is disrespecting his mother. He reminded me, "My mother will always make the best chicken curry." I agreed and said that I hoped to taste it some day. He said that he will always love her the most. I told him that makes sense, but that love need not be a competition. He told me she will always be his mother. I said always and held him tight.

Then, as is typical for Adrian, his questions got even harder, his analysis even sharper. "But," he said, "wasn't my mother taking such a risk, sending me to you? She didn't even know you. She had never even met you." I have thought about that many times, but hadn't thought yet about what I might say when he asked that question. How did that happen? Why did that happen and what does it mean? To some extent, the way Grace handed Adrian to me is common among African Americans, since Grace did not involve the state in the process. Also, Adrian was sent from his mother to me without a lot of conversation about whether or not Grace was abandoning Adrian. Grace did not frame the separation that way at all.

On the other hand, this handoff is not common because most of the time it is done to someone who is very well known within the community — typically within the same ethnic community. But Grace had never laid eyes on me. She did, however, know of me through the years I had been loving Andrea. Grace knew I had hung in there with Andrea. Gone to her crew races. Bought her clothes. Been with her on school vacations, Christmas, Thanksgiving, and more. She knows I love Andrea. But Grace has never met me herself. She sent her son on an airplane halfway across the country for a vacation with a white woman she had never met and then called up a week later to ask if I could keep Adrian for the long run. Adrian knew this part of the story. That he came on an airplane. That his mother initiated the conversation about his staying. What we had not yet talked about was whether his mother took a risk, from his perspective an enormous risk — sending him to someone she barely knew, had never even met.

Actually, Grace had done some temporary handoffs in the past that weren't good for Adrian — leaving him for ten days with a friend of hers while not telling either her friend or Adrian that she was leaving or when she would return. After that "extended visit," Adrian landed for a few months in a foster home in Louisiana, for reasons I still haven't learned, until his grandmother came and got him and the younger children.

But the boy sitting next to me in bed, with his two friends in the next room, is asking me incredibly difficult questions. Should I walk him through the times she left him with others as a way to show that, yes, it *is* a risk? Should I then say that this risk was worth it, especially in comparison to those other handoffs? Might I then undermine the support I have been giving to the idea that she has tried to take good care of Adrian? I have been trying hard not to take Grace down, while supporting him when he starts to doubt his idealized image of her.

So, in that moment of Adrian's unexpected questions, I left out details. I left out a conversation about how this time was different from the others — that the others were temporary reactions under duress, while this one was a planned action that is long term. I left out myriad examples of Grace's putting Adrian and Andrea at risk in the past. I didn't bring up the times that Damion beat Adrian with belts or his fists while Grace stood by silently. I left out the many times Grace left Adrian to care for his two younger siblings, even when Adam was still a baby.

I left out the example of Grace's pulling Andrea out of her second year of college with the promise that Grace would leave her husband and go to a treatment center for battered women. Andrea dropped out of school and moved to Louisiana to care for Adrian and his younger brother and sister. In November, before finals, she withdrew, jeopardizing her whole semester. She quickly learned when she arrived in Louisiana that Damion was still living with Grace. Grace had not begun a battered women's program, as she had promised. Damion was hell-bent on beating her up as well as Adrian and Andrea. Fearing for her life, Andrea finally left after working three jobs while her mother was at home with the children. Andrea finally left after she had intervened many times when Damion was beating Adrian up, after Damion had lashed out at Andrea again and again.

Adrian still hasn't forgiven Andrea for leaving him there with Damion that time. He still thinks Andrea abandoned him when she caught a ride with members of the university crew team back to school in March. To this day, he still sees Grace as the silent victim and Andrea as the one who abandoned him. Andrea left after filing a police report against Damion and vowing to herself that she would come back for Adrian as soon as she could. She did that several months later, when she took a bus to New York City, picked Adrian up, and brought him to visit Ella and me for the first time at Thanksgiving.

But last night, with Adrian asking, "Don't you think that my mother took quite a risk to send me to you?" I skipped those details and many others. I skipped trying to explain his mother's logic or how Andrea fit into the picture. Instead, I turned to Adrian, who had snuggled up as close to me as possible and said, "I am definitely not a risk. Not at all. I am the real thing. A sure shot. I can give you what you need. And I am. Intellectually. Spiritually. Emotionally. And more." Silence from his side of the bed. Big breathing. And then from him, "I miss my mother so much." Big sobs. I rocked him, feeling great tenderness in my heart. I said again that it was good he was talking about it. That we need to talk about it. Then I said, "When you came to me, I became able to pass some of the love your mother has for you to you. I can be a medium for her love. A part of your mother is in me." He said, "And a part of you is in her, too." "Yes, I think that is true," I agreed.

I put my hand on his heart and began to feel energy pass from my hand to his warm body. "Maybe," I said, "we could try feeling her love together." Silence from his side of the bed. Big quiet. His regular breathing. More quiet. Stillness in the air. Then, a couple of minutes later, from Adrian, "Isn't love powerful?" "Yes it is, Adrian," I whispered back. "I can feel the stars at night," he told me, "when I look out the window." "I am going to sleep here tonight, okay?" "Sure, Adrian. Just don't push me off the bed." "Okay," he said. I heard his heavy breathing soon. Then deep sleep from him.

I held him during and after he drifted off, hoping, some-how believing, that I could channel some of his mother's love to him. I lay there, wondering what she might think of that concept, she who goes to church on Saturdays, she who is a Seventh-Day Adventist. I lay awake wondering, hoping, that someday she and I might find a way to talk about god and raising children from a place of spiritual faith. No rush though. Neither one of us has wanted to go too fast in finding out where we agree or where we disagree, about anything and everything.

In "Mothering across Racial and Cultural Boundaries," Shelley Park writes, "The best way to provide the adopted child of color with a sense of personal as well as racial and ethnic identity is to provide her with the opportunity to know her birth parents. This is also the best way to exemplify respect for and build sisterhood with the birth mother."[3] Adrian will certainly know his birth mother — who was his only mother for his first nine years of life. But how Grace and I come to know each other and how I learn to respond to Adrian's questions about love, tenderness, and maternal connection will make a huge difference in how well she and I will be able to walk him through this process. In these months so far, Grace has been giving me the lead in all regards, mostly, I guess, because she has been just too overwhelmed to do otherwise. Maybe she also knows that I need to take the lead now, since he is living with me, day after day, and, I hope, for the duration.

Sex education in the 1990s

Sᴇx ᴇᴅᴜᴄᴀᴛɪᴏɴ ʙᴇɢᴀɴ ɪɴ ᴛʜɪs ғᴀᴍɪʟʏ in the fall, when Adrian and I were eating breakfast with Hannah and her daughter, Diana, at a local diner in Brookline — the Busy Bee, known for its fast short-order cooks, home fries made with real potatoes, and caustic and fearless waitresses. Once Adrian came, Hannah and I often took the kids to breakfast on Saturday mornings, partly to avoid having to cook or clean up. Mostly, though, we went after having realized that over meals, especially at restaurants, Adrian tended to bring up the hard stuff, raise the real issues, and offer the dirt on his latest quandaries.

Diana and Adrian jostled about which toys to bring into the restaurant and who would sit on the outside and inside seat of the lime green, Naugahyde booth. After we ordered the food, which Adrian considers the essential business, he asked me if two men could kiss. I asked him if both of them were at least sixteen. He said "Yes," he thought so. "Are both of them consenting as well? Do they both want to kiss?" I asked. "Yes," Adrian said with a humph, looking at me with one of those why-do-you-have-to-use-such-complicated-language looks. "Well, if they are consenting and old enough, then they can go for it," I said back to Adrian.

Adrian looks at Diana, Diana looks at Adrian, then Diana says, "That is what my mom and Becky do. They kiss." Diana continues with total clarity, "You know, a girl doing it with another girl. That means they are gay." Adrian looks at Diana, then at me, then at Hannah. He then points at Hannah and says in an incredulous whisper, "You? You're a lesbian?" "Yes," Hannah says calmly, with the confidence born of twenty-plus years of being an out lesbian with various long-term relationships along the way. Adrian says, "What?!" rolls his eyes, starts to stick his finger down his throat, and pretends to gag. My heart stops beating, totally unprepared for such a visceral reaction, not knowing that, at his age, he might well have mimicked choking with the mention of any kind of adult sexuality. For him and most other fourth-grade boys, sexuality is "just disgusting."

I reach over to Adrian, touch him lightly on his arm, and say, "It's okay. We can talk about it." I touch him, probably to assure myself as much as or more than him. Diana points to her mother and says, "Yeah, she's a lesbian," and then points to me — waving her finger back and forth, between Hannah and me — until Adrian figures out that if Hannah is a lesbian, and I am her partner, then I must be a lesbian, too. Hannah and I look at each other, smiling, trying not to burst into laughter, outed at a local breakfast diner in Boston by an eight-year-old girl who has been surrounded, since she was adopted as a toddler, by lesbians who love her — her mother and her mother's many friends.

The kids go back to their toys as I sit, worrying silently about how Adrian will now use this information. Hating that is where my mind goes. Will he somehow know *not* to bring it up during one of his weekly phone conversations with his mother? It is too risky for me to find out if she is homophobic, at least until I have the guardianship papers that, at that point, were still pending. I look at Hannah with searching eyes. Though we are obviously not able to have this conversation now, I desperately need Hannah to see my fear, so I am not alone with homophobia potentially aimed at Adrian and me.

During Gay Pride Week at Silver Street School, the teachers offered children a number of ways to learn about gay and lesbian life, including conversations about famous gay authors and artists, a discussion of lesbian and gay families, and a talk about the school's commitment to justice and equality. Between the morning at the Busy Bee restaurant and the scheduled assembly honoring the gay men and lesbians at Silver Street School, Adrian had come home with a vocabulary sheet requiring him and me to look up many words together — "lesbian," "homophobia," "discrimination," "sexuality," "equality," "protest," and "heterosexism" — and to use them in sentences. We did the assignment sprawled out with a big red dictionary that I have been using since I was in college.

He loved that I knew so much about the subject, that I could tell him definitions that went beyond the ones in the dictionary. Yes, as we discovered, the dictionary says a lesbian is "a native or resident of Lesbos, an island of Greece." "That is true, Adrian," I tell him. "But there are also lesbians in Nigeria, where your uncle Kayode is from, and South Africa, where I have traveled recently, and Mexico, where your housemate is from, and Brazil, where women—lesbian and straight—wear bikinis that are so brief that 'why bother?'

"Yes, you are right, Adrian. 'Heterosexism' is not in this dictionary. Let's look at when this dictionary was published," I say, while showing him how to find the date of publication on a left-hand page close to the front of the book. First in 1969. Last edition in 1981. "Well," I tell him, "it would make sense that 'heterosexism' would not be in the dictionary in 1969. That was the same year as Stonewall, which is considered the beginning of the gay liberation movement in the United States, when a multira-cial group of gays and lesbians, many of them drag queens and butches, took to the streets in protest of police harass-ment in bars in New York City. Close to where you were born in fact, Adrian, almost twenty years before you were born." Ancient history in his mind.

"It makes sense," I explain, "that the earlier editions wouldn't include a definition of 'heterosexism' since the social movement was just beginning then. But why not in the 1980s?" I ask Adrian. "There is really no excuse," he explains. "That is an example of heterosexism." I beam at him as he uses the term "heterosexism" correctly and in context.

As we work our way through the list, Adrian asks many questions: "When did you know you were a lesbian?" "How could Hannah be a lesbian, too? She's too old." In his mind, Hannah's age—fifty-four—seems to put her out of range of being sexual. So, I let him know that for many people—including Hannah and me—getting older makes them more, not less, in touch with their sexuality, desire, and whom they love.

By the time the assembly honoring gay and lesbian awareness day came to Silver Street, I had clearly come to be a status symbol—albeit a temporary one—in Adrian's mind. As an out lesbian at the school, I was someone Adrian could claim that week. Because of me, he had special knowledge—the insider's scoop. Because of me, he would definitely have a special reason to be at the assembly. Because of our conversation, he had, so the teachers told me later, the confidence to talk more in class that week than he had so far during the fall.

I marvel at how it is that Adrian came to understand my sexuality first through a gay- and lesbian-friendly curriculum at his school. And how that timing was so unique to our particular situation. Had he been living with me longer, his knowledge about lesbians might have first been through his being teased by his peers. Chances are his first interactions might have begun on the defensive—having to protect himself and me from teasing or to separate from me in some painful way.

Before he came to Silver Street, I think he knew very little. I had said almost nothing to him, believing that he would ask when he was ready. I was hesitant about being explicit for fear that he might talk about it with his mother or grandmother before I was ready. My heart was very full the day of the assembly as parents filed in to watch the event. An eclectic and colorful group of parents had made it their business to come—straight, lesbian, gay, and bisexual. And the children clearly seemed joyful about this day of celebration.

Most important of all for me, though, was how the week on gay and lesbian lives helped Adrian find a way to talk with me about race and racism for the first time. It

was when he asked me about examples of heterosexism
that he first offered his own feelings about racism. It was
when I said that not everyone can be counted on to deal
well with issues of prejudice against gays and lesbians that
he talked about not trusting very many people to understand the isolation and hurt he feels as an African American
child. In my college classes, I teach about the power of
bridge work—how knowing about one oppression can,
in some situations, lead people to want to learn about other
oppressions. But to see Adrian reach toward his knowledge
of racism to let me know that he understood heterosexism,
to see that his outrage when I told him about gay-bashing
could help him see why I would feel outrage about racist
violence, convinced me like never before of the power of
bridge work as a translator of experience.

The second sex education lesson came this week, nine
months into our life together, following a day of discussion
in Adrian's class about "the human body." The teachers
had told me during our last parent-teacher conference that
they would talk soon with the children about bodies. I
stored this information along with unwritten shopping
lists, dates of upcoming birthday parties, and information
about car-pool schedules. I knew the conversation had
begun when, at our biweekly dinner with Issac, Adrian
asks, seemingly out of the blue, how sperm reach the egg.
I grab a napkin so I can draw a picture of a woman's
ovaries, fallopian tubes, uterus, and vagina, and I begin
explaining how each month the uterus makes a soft cushiony nest in case the sperm and egg meet. I tell Adrian
about how each month a meeting doesn't take place, a
woman's body knows to send that nest on its way out
of her in order to start over. Adrian squirms in his chair,

wanting to ask and not wanting to ask at the same time, as I try to get Issac's attention.

Issac shuffles in his chair, obviously uncomfortable about this conversational turn of events. When Adrian leaves the room for a few minutes, I turn to Issac and say, "When Adrian comes back, will you add what you think about all of this? I think it is no coincidence that Adrian is bringing up conversations about sex in your presence. Adrian probably wants a man here as his witness as he asks questions. My guess is that Adrian wouldn't bring these questions up with me alone. Will you talk about this with us?"

Issac looks up at me meekly and says, "I'll try. But I didn't talk about this with my own kids you know. My wife did all that." When Adrian returns, Issac starts talking slowly. "Well, Adrian, love is this romantic thing that can happen between two people. It can be painful and exciting. Love is what really matters in it all." Adrian looks back at Issac funny. I look at Adrian, look at Issac, and think to myself: such a typical Issac response. This man who has taught courses on birth and death from a literary and spiritual perspective for more than thirty years, who is now bypassing issues of biology to get to matters of the heart. But then I think, I don't want Adrian to think we are avoiding his questions about s-e-x. I take a breath and then start in. "While I agree wholeheartedly that love is the bottom line, what I think you are asking for, Adrian, is bare-bones information about sex, the human body, how things work, and don't work." Now Issac begins to squirm in his chair. He is clearly willing to sit and listen, but unwilling to talk himself about penises and vaginas around his dinner table. A generational divide? Perhaps. A question of manners? Perhaps. Regardless, Adrian keeps asking questions, perhaps satisfied with Issac as a silent companion, not needing Issac to say anything, but just to be there as his witness.

Adrian tells me that he is too embarrassed to ask more. I keep smiling while telling him that he could be interested and embarrassed and even, in his words, "disgusted" all at the same time. All those things could happen at once, I let him know. Adrian grins, obviously caught feeling all of those emotions simultaneously and relieved at making that common knowledge.

Adrian continues with his list of questions, wanting to know how lesbians make babies. I tell him first about adoption: "Some don't even make kids, Adrian. They just get them. Like me getting you, already nine years old, almost five feet tall now, but once just the size of one microscopic sperm and one microscopic egg." "How else do lesbians have kids?" Adrian asks, clearly looking for another answer, obviously aware of adoption as a way lesbians become moms. "Well," I explain, "some lesbians have sex the old-fashioned way with men they know, men they love, or men they have no interest in ever seeing again." Adrian looks at me with one of those "oh-brother-I-already-know-this" looks, clearly seeking another answer.

"How else? How else? What about sperm?" he asks, as I search his face for a clue to what he is looking for. Finally, it dawns on me that he must have heard something about sperm banks already and wants to know more. "Well," I ponder, "it is true, Adrian, that some lesbians go to a clinic where they have these vials of semen with sperm from different men and you can actually specify — African American, white, old, young, a musician, a carpenter. Crazy, isn't it, Adrian, that level of specificity?" "Am I going to get a younger brother or sister?" he asks. Then, before I can begin to answer, he continues, "Would you go to a sperm bank and what would you ask for?" Not yet sure what I would say myself, I turn the tables back on him. "What would you specify?" I ask. He gives me another quizzical look, another laughing smile, and then asks, "Well, when a lesbian goes to a sperm bank, does she pay the bank or does the bank pay her?"

Only in the 1990s, I find myself thinking, could this be happening. A nine-year-old who considers a conversation about sperm banks as part of the discussion of how babies get born. Only because of the education provided at a sex education–friendly school and through the life Adrian is leading, surrounded by lesbians, would he know to initiate conversations about sperm banks as an integral part of a discussion about conception and birth.

After Adrian polishes off three pieces of fruit and all of the Bermans' ice cream, we drive home to conversations on other subjects. But clearly Adrian is not done. Over hot chocolate, Adrian starts in on more questions. "How does a penis get inside of a vagina?" he asks forthrightly. "Well, Adrian, the penis gets bigger as a man gets excited," I say. I take a big breath and begin demonstrating with my right hand, as my fingers get stronger and straighter and head toward my left hand, which I have partially cupped to cover my fingers on my right hand. "Meanwhile," I explain, "a woman's vagina gets excited and a little wet. As the two people rub and touch and maybe talk to each other, if there is love and tenderness in the air, both keep getting excited to the point where a woman's vagina starts to expand, starts to make way until a man's penis fits inside it like a hand in a glove. Then sometimes the two people start to moan, sounds that tell each other it feels good."

"So," Adrian asks, "what happens next, if when *that*," as he points to my right hand, which is now cupped inside my partially closed left hand, "gets enclosed in *that?*" — pointing to my left hand. With my hands as his living diagram, he has found a way to continue to ask questions without having to say the words "vagina" or "penis." "Well, a woman is able to squeeze a man's penis with her muscles in a way that feels really good until the man comes," I say. "Sometimes the woman comes too at that point. But not usually, since what really makes a woman have an orgasm is when her clitoris is touched in an erotic way." "Clitoris?" Adrian asks, clearly not having heard of that before. I steam inside. How could the teachers not have told him about a clitoris if they have already talked about penises? Adrian continues to ask more questions: "What does that look like? Where is it? What does it like?" I explain as best as I can, about this little area that lies inside a woman's lips that feels a little like the tip of a nose, that gets a little bigger and fuller and brighter as it gets excited. "A clitoris is kind of like a pinball machine on a microchip. When a clitoris gets excited, it can go ping-ping-ping-ping, like what happens when you score on a pinball machine." "So then," Adrian asks, "how do lesbians make love? How does that work?" "Two clitorises," I explain. "Twice the fun. Lots of room for touch and teasing." Big eyes he gives me. Smiling shyly. Tells me again that he is so embarrassed. "Makes sense," I say. "Hard questions and good questions," I reassure him. "You can be embarrassed and interested at the same time."

"So," he asks, obviously building to the most interesting questions to him, "How does a penis get bigger, and, if it comes, won't it run out of semen?" "A lot of times a penis gets bigger if a man strokes himself," I tell him. "Plays with himself. By himself. It can feel good. Some people do that, Adrian. Not everyone plays with himself or herself in their lives. I think I never did, partly because of being sexually abused. But many people do play with themselves and like it. And no, Adrian, a man won't run out of semen. A man can make more, and quickly. It is kind of like watery milk. It is soft."

Smiles from him. Relaxation on his face as he is clearly enjoying that he has managed to make me let him stay up past his bedtime by asking such good questions. Sex education in the nineties, when questions about lesbian love and sperm banks seem as relevant to Adrian as questions about men and women making each other hot. Sex education in the nineties, when sexual abuse and violation assume a necessary place in the discussion. Sex education in the nineties with a child who, on the one hand, had never heard of a clitoris. On the other hand, he never once asked me if he should talk with his mother about my being a lesbian until the day after I was granted permanent guardianship. A kid who somehow has been figuring out what is safe to talk about and what isn't. A kid who has been figuring out how discretion is a necessary response to heterosexism in many situations, including this one.

Sex education in the 1990s, with a child whose boundaries seem to be so much more secure and in place than mine were at his age. Sex education in the 1990s, when the feminist movement, *Our Bodies, Ourselves,* and the lesbian and gay movement have made possible a conversation between us that complements the one he is getting at school. A conversation that contradicts misinformation. That gives Adrian a running start on understanding how his body is changing, and fast, as we buy him a size eight and a half men's shoe in the men's section of Foot Locker, less than nine months after he was fitted with a size six shoe at the Stride Rite store for children. A 1990s conversation that doesn't yet deal with the politics of race in an upfront way, but that will need to as time goes on. These are 1990s conversations Adrian has initiated that, for a flutter of a second, make me hopeful.

In *The Fire Next Time,* James Baldwin writes, "[White Americans] are terrified of sensuality and do not any longer understand it. The word 'sensual' is not intended to bring to mind quivering dusky maidens or priapic Black studs. I am referring to something much simpler and much less fanciful. To be sensual, I think, is to respect and rejoice in the force of life, of life itself, and to be *present* in all that one does, from the effort of loving to the breaking of bread."[1] Adrian seems to already get Baldwin's words. May that force in him remain and grow.

So grown

"He'll need a men's size nine sneakers," the shoe salesman tells me as I look at Adrian's feet aghast. I begin chasing him around the store, accusing him of deliberately refusing to take his shrinking medicine regularly. He gallops away from me, dodging the Foot Locker displays, clearly enjoying the latest in a series of public announcements that he is growing very fast. About two months after he came, I started to feel deep pangs about all that I had missed, wondering what he had looked like when he was three years old, when he first got a full head of hair, whether his skin color now was the color behind his ears from the beginning or whether the rest of his skin caught up with that color over time.

There are no remaining photographs of Adrian or Andrea when they were small children. Andrea had one precious box of photos and cherished letters, which she had left with her mother when she went away to school. But that box somehow disappeared, and with it, all historical documentation of Adrian's and Andrea's lives. So, we don't even have pictures. I wonder how I can help Adrian chronicle his life, especially now, as I am assembling a photo album to help celebrate his one-year anniversary

since I began mothering him. I yearn for photographs of
his past, as a way to, at least through pictures, know how
his little hands felt, how his little feet looked, how his eyes
looked in the bathtub or when he spit out yams when he
was still a baby.

This is why I have been routinely telling him that shrinking medicine is in order—that he must grow backward
for a while before he can grow tall again. This is why I
have threatened him with, "No, I won't allow you to leave
for college ever! After high school, you won't be allowed
out of the house at all except to walk the dogs." He smiles
and jokes whenever I raise this threat. "Yes," he tells me,
he fully intends to leave then, with at least one dog at his
side. I smile inside, watching him settle into knowing that
I intend to be with him through the fifth, sixth, seventh,
eighth, ninth, tenth, eleventh, *and* twelfth grades. That
this is a permanent arrangement—at least until he is fully
grown—and then some, if he wants.

The dilemmas of starting this life at the half leave me
staring into space in the aisle of Foot Locker, until I hear
Adrian inform me that the Michael Jordan sneakers are
not only the coolest looking, but the best made. He looks
up at me with his most woeful, pitiful look, no doubt hoping that his reasoning might somehow seem believable
and sensible to me. I give him one of my sternist, pretend
faces as we go to the sales rack to pick out the third pair
of sneakers in three months. It's not just three boxes of
cereal each week. It's the sneakers, too.

It is my pride and fear about his growing, both in the
same instant, that filled my eyes with happy tears this week
when, for the first time, he outran me in touch football
and then scored a touchdown. Not only had he caught the

ball despite my real attempt to intercept it; he had also run
right past me, even though, as I admitted only to myself, I
was going at top speed. I yearn for the little boy he was
when he came to me, with his one suitcase and his round,
round belly. I am loving the big person he is becoming, the
expansive, soon-to-be-teenage boy, even as I grieve about
how my chance to know him from the beginning has long
since passed.

I was awed by Adrian's growth, and by the sudden
piercing realization that he neither came through me nor
belongs to me as I somehow drove away after saying good-
bye to him at his first day of a three-week overnight camp.
His first overnight camp. My first as well. I, full of anxiety,
anger, energy, fear. He, so determined to learn all the sports
he never got to play until this year. He, so intent his first
day of camp that I not interrupt him so he could pitch the
kickball to the next person waiting at home plate. I looked
at him, so strong and tall, with the summer tan that has
made his skin even richer. I marveled at his tenacity, hugged
him good-bye, and headed toward my car.

Not an easy task, driving away, however. We arrived
at the camp on a sunny summer Sunday along with my
naive assumption that the junior camp set up for ten- and
eleven-year-olds would mirror the high school program
where Andrea works. I assumed that the junior program,
like the senior program, would feel international, and that
there would be a critical mass of children of color. I thought
I would hear many languages spoken on the volleyball
courts and in the dining halls, as I had become used to in
the program for the high school students. Instead, in the
first two hours at the junior camp, I saw only two Black
families among what felt like hundreds of white families

getting out of their Explorers, Saabs, Volvos, and other jet-setter cars.

At first, I told myself that the African American families might come for the second, rather than the first, informational session. But when two o'clock turned to four o'clock and I still saw no more Black families, it began to sink in that I had enrolled Adrian in a summer camp that was as lily white as they come. Worse, I hadn't even warned him of this reality. In the time I was there, I also saw no parent who even remotely looked lesbian or gay to me — not that we can always recognize each other, but even one obvious dyke family would have helped.

As I sat through the "highly recommended" informational session led by the camp director for the parents of campers, I listened to questions about whether the children would get to use phone cards, if wood shop would include training in the table saw as well as the radial saw, and whether the children could write to their parents via E-mail as well as the old-fashioned way. Meanwhile, I found my heart beating harder and harder as I realized that, yes, I was going to need to ask a question about race and racism. Somehow, having the conversation stay at the level of table saws and phone cards, when Adrian was going to be one of only a handful of children of color in the whole camp, was just too much for me.

I felt myself start to sweat, big drops running down my T-shirt sleeves, as I wondered how I could ask a question in a way that would put race and racism into the auditorium space without leading the program director to draw back and become defensive. I wondered how to ask about ways the staff deals with the isolation that children of color will inevitably feel, without the director then somehow taking it out on Adrian, exceptionalizing him, labeling me a troublemaker or the two of us ungrateful for Adrian's full scholarship. I found myself scanning the audience for the two Black families I had seen earlier and wondered if sitting by them would somehow diminish my nervousness. Maybe yes, maybe no. They could say, "How naive she is to think that raising the issue will do any good," or "Look at that bold white woman speaking out about racism." Or they could think, "Why is she going on and on about this?" Who even knows what they would think? I had met neither family and had not a clue about their racial politics.

I found myself wondering how Frederick Douglass continued to speak up in potentially hostile environments for so many years of his life, even as I knew that his speaking was far riskier than mine would ever be. Did the white antiracist activists Anne Braden and Lillian Smith notice their hearts pounding when they tried to interrupt the invisibility of whiteness and speak to the inevitability of racism in all white contexts? "This is just one small, slight intervention," I reasoned, "No big deal. Just raise your hand," which I did, finally, at the tail end of the meeting, after people were already getting restless.

I raised my hand and waited as a few more people asked their questions until the director motioned in my direction. I took a big breath and tried to say coolly and calmly that, as the mother of an African American ten-year-old boy, I was concerned about how racism in the camp was dealt with. I heard myself asking how the staff dealt with issues of diversity. "I hate that phrase," I thought to myself as the words came out of my mouth anyway. How did the staff deal with the isolation that inevitably comes up for children of color in overwhelmingly white settings and the racism that they face? As I spoke, I felt several people's eyes drop around me, look down toward the floor, as the formerly bustling, restless room went totally silent.

The director took a big breath and then started down a dangerous path, telling me that the camp had children with disabilities as well as children of color, that children are taught that "not everyone is the same. Some kids are different." I thought to myself, am I going to have to take her out in the back alley myself? How can she, in the 1990s, be making a comparison between an African American boy and a child with a disability — as if being Black is a disability? As if disability is the difference, is the problem, rather than the second-floor dorm rooms that no wheelchair could ever get up to. As if white people are the norm, while people of color are "different" — even though people of color are seven-eighths of the world's population.

Don't go down that road, I silently reasoned with her. Take another tack. Change your approach, which she did, after her first stumble. She continued by saying that, yes, the staff are trained to recognize when children are being racist. And they immediately call children in who have said something racist. It was good, at least, that she had switched the conversation from Adrian begin the "difference," the "problem," to white racism being the problem. She also talked about how there were more students of color in the camp than met the eye. Many of the day campers are children of color, she explained, since parents of color are much more willing to send their children away for the day than for three weeks.

I sat there, sitting on my hands, wondering why I was just now learning this information. Why hadn't I done my homework? Why was I just now seeing the all-white com-

position of the campers? Why hadn't I warned Adrian?
What was going to happen when he started to hear homophobic comments from fellow campers? Not that he didn't
hear them at his school this year. No place is immune from
rude, fear-filled comments. But at his school, one of his
teachers is a lesbian. Many of the children come from gay
and lesbian families. Adrian has been in a pretty protected
environment this year, being raised by many people, some
of whom are not only lesbians but butch lesbians, who are
readily identifiable as lesbians. A village of people have
taken him to the movies, made a huge deal out of his birthday, Christmas, Valentine's Day, Passover, and the many
days that were made into holidays just for the fun of it.
He has been living in a multiracial community with color
all around him—at school and at home and in the neighborhood. And now this. A lily-white camp where I don't
even see many Jewish families. Help. I am drowning. What
do I do? Is he tall enough, strong enough, ready enough
to be the only Black kid, the only kid from a lesbian family,
the only kid with a Caribbean mom in Idaho and a white
mom in Boston?

At the end of his therapy session this week with his
African American therapist, the therapist and Adrian
asked me to come into the office for a play they had prepared about going to camp. With a couch pushed out
from the wall so it could be used as the stage, they performed a five-act play with eight stuffed animals. The
lead of the play was a small stuffed turtle camper whose
voice and personality were distinctly similar to Adrian's.
It turns out that the stuffed turtle puppet had made it very
clear that if any of the counselors hurt his feelings or his
person, he would eat them. On the spot. In act three, the

stuffed turtle puppet met another camper—this one a
stuffed moose, who was a few years younger than the
stuffed turtle and, not surprisingly, looked up to the turtle
as if he were god's gift to the animal king/queendom. The
turtle and the moose became good friends, played basketball together (with, of course, the turtle outscoring the
moose), and hugged and exchanged addresses at the end
of camp. By the end of the three-week camp session,
when the mother stuffed turtle came to pick up the little
turtle, none of the camp counselor stuffed animals had
been eaten.

Adrian loved performing the five-act play, especially
since the therapist had let the session run over a full half
hour because Adrian said the play needed to be five acts,
not three. Adrian loved having figured out a way to be in
control of the counselors—to threaten them with canni-
balism. I laughed and laughed at the therapist's playfulness,
as he stretched himself into all sorts of contorted positions
to hold innumerable stuffed animals up on the couch stage
for lengthy stretches of time, as he kept his right hand
inside the mommy turtle puppet for five long acts, and as
he took cues from Adrian the whole time.

When Adrian and I arrived at the camp, we went
straight to his room to "set up," as he and I had done with
Andrea the week before, when we took her to the counselors' orientation week at the senior program. As I had
done previous years when Andrea had gone off to camp
or to another year away at school, I had brought incense,
to bless the room from the four corners to the center of
the space. Adrian, Andrea, and I had set up her whole room
in just a few minutes—made her bed, put her wigs on

hooks for her gender-bending course, and plugged in her stereo, so Ani DiFranco could sing us through the ritual.

When Adrian and I arrived at the junior camp, he wanted to do the same thing, announcing, "Let's do the altar first." My eyes grew big when he said that. So much my child in wanting to do that first, except that he came to me last year already thinking that way. He had asked for an altar for his room the first week he arrived last summer. We set up the altar in his dorm room, with photos of Andrea and Adrian, Adrian and his uncle Kayode, and Adrian and me, surrounded by several of his carefully selected stuffed animals.

We looked around the room for hints of who his roommate might be, both of us hoping that his roommate would be Black. In came Henry and his family, friendly, open, happy to meet Adrian, and clearly an Irish family through and through. We all said hello. Adrian and I turned back to setting up the altar. I asked Adrian if he wanted Mighty, his stuffed turtle, to have his head inside or outside his shell. At home, Mighty's head is always outside, as he sits on Adrian's shelf, "so he doesn't miss a trick," Adrian has told me. Adrian looked at me, his face closed and nervous since the new roommate arrived, since he clearly noticed that every child we had seen unloading their stuff from their cars, hanging out in the quad, and registering for the first day had been white, including his roommate. Adrian turned to me and said, "Put Mighty's head in for now. He can stay on the altar, but he wants to be inside his shell today. I'll check on him later."

Brave boy, I thought to myself. Tall boy. Big feeling boy. On his own for three weeks. So good at making

friends. So eager to learn anything and everything. So
much wanting to succeed at camp—to please his big sister,
who had pushed him to go since the fall. Having to be
brave now, and I hadn't prepared him. I should have prepared him. Not that it would have changed things, but at
least we could have talked about it together.

I tied a beaded bracelet with the South African flag col-
ors around his wrist and told him that I'd be with him
through the bracelet—morning, noon, and night. We finished putting away his clothes as he told me that he wanted
to join the kickball game. "Let's go," he said. The night
before, after dinner, he had turned to me and said, "You
know how the last bloom on a rose is the most beautiful?
Well, that is how you are for me. The last bloom." I
blessed his dorm room as I had Andrea's. He sat on the
bed and waited for me to bless him last. I kissed his
pregma—the top chakra above the forehead, just above
the hairline. I told him I loved him. We ran outside together
as he reminded me that he beat me on the football field the
day before—"in sandals," he said. "I didn't even have my
sneakers on and I beat you." I told him, "You are making
it up. I don't know who you are talking about. I will
always outrun you." He grinned, knowing my lie, as I felt
him grow taller and taller in front of my eyes.

I watched him run toward the kickball game. I walked
across the long, long grassy fields toward my car at the
edge of a big, big grassy sports field—the kind that makes
private schools in New England seem so wealthy and so
overwhelming to me. I put my head on the steering wheel
to say a silent prayer—to give thanks for this amazing
boy who has come into my life. I asked the universe to
protect him and love him during the time he is away from

me. I put on Aretha Franklin's *One Faith* tape, which she recorded in her father's church, and I fast-forwarded to the Mighty Clouds of Joy's song, "I Have Been in the Storm Too Long."

I know that I have barely been in the storm. Adrian is in the center of one now. May the eye of the hurricane find him, and may he stay in its calm center for the three weeks to come. May he and I find the language when he comes back to talk about everything together. May he not try to protect me from what was hard. May he be able to feel fully and have many hugs from loving people while he is there. May he know that the rest of his stuffed animals are waiting for him when he gets back.

A friend of mine who suffered brain damage four years ago from a terrible car crash and has needed to start her life over again recently said that she thinks one of the most important lessons you can teach a child is impermanence. I tell her that with all the moving and loss and instability of my childhood, that lesson seems harsh to me. "Impermanence," she tells me, "is different from instability. Adrian needs stability and you are giving that to him. Impermanence means accepting that the only real constancy is change." I put my head on the steering wheel and say my prayers. I drive out of the grassy field, past the kickball game. Somehow, in a matter of minutes between my saying good-bye to Adrian and my getting to the car, he has become the pitcher, the absolute center of the game. I honk enough to make a fool of myself. He barely looks up, already completely immersed in the game. So tall. So big. So grown.

Sand beneath my feet, the tide takes its turn

From the time Adrian came to live with me a
little over a year ago until I got the permanent guardianship papers, I often had to talk myself out of feeling panic
at the possibility of losing him. Until I had the permanent
guardianship, anyone from Adrian's family — his mother,
Grace, or his stepfather, or his grandmother, or his uncle,
David — could come get him any time and I could do nothing to stop them. To calm myself, I would go over the many
reasons that would probably not happen.

Adrian's grandmother, Grace's mother, had protested
loudly to Grace before she had signed the guardianship
papers, saying that such an act proved that Grace did not
love Adrian, did not want to protect Adrian, and was a
very bad parent. His grandmother had chosen to be out
of the house, out of her own house in New York, the day
my friend Ella had driven there to deliver the guardianship
papers to Grace. The grandmother's own form of absentia,
I guess, after the accusation she made, did little to dissuade
Grace. But I really didn't think that the grandmother would
claim Adrian. She had already raised several of her own
children and had taken care of her grandchildren many
times in the past for extended periods. Adrian hadn't heard

from his grandmother even by phone all through the fall, winter, and into the spring, except for the time Andrea happened to call her grandmother while she was staying in Boston for a long weekend.

I also didn't think that Adrian's Uncle David would claim Adrian. He already had his hands full—going to school to get his B.A. so he could someday apply to medical school, and working full time as a janitor to help support his mother, himself, and probably others in the family. Adrian and Andrea always spoke of David as someone they looked up to—hardworking, sweet to the degree that he sometimes took care of others before himself (including dropping out of college, as Andrea had done, so he could make more money for the family). Years ago, David had given Adrian a pair of his old plaid pajamas, which then must have been huge on Adrian. By the time I first saw the pajamas, they had several tears and were still way too long on Adrian. But he hung on to those pajamas like there was no tomorrow, wearing the bottoms over his feet like infant snuggle pajamas. I didn't worry that David might come for Adrian, although I sometimes wondered why he never called—whether calling would seem to him like a betrayal of his mother's protest of Grace's decision to send Adrian to me.

Adrian worried that his stepfather Damion might come get him—not to take him away, but to hurt him. He worried about that a lot. Sometimes when he was awake, I could tell that he was feeling afraid when his eyebrows would furrow and he'd get a look of panic on his face. "Adrian, what's wrong?" I would ask him. "I thought I saw Damion walking down the street," he would tell me with terror spiking his voice. Or, "Damion could find our

address, you know. He could just show up here some day."
I know that Adrian worried at night, too — in dreams,
sometimes turned to nightmares, that would wake him
up and send him running into my room. I worried for
Adrian — that he was haunted by the memories of such a
cruel man, whose cruelty, I had begun to suspect, was even
worse than the memories Adrian had told me about. But I
didn't worry that Damion would be the one to take Adrian
away from me. Damion was too self-centered, too caught
up in abusing Grace, and too local in his thinking to make
his way from Idaho to Boston.

If anyone was going to come get Adrian between the
time he came to me and the time I got the permanent
papers, it would have been his mother. That sometimes
did scare me. Maybe Grace's mother would persuade her
that, by definition, sending Adrian to me made her a bad
mother. Maybe in the loneliest of lonely times, in the times
when Grace had left Damion (before going back again),
she would remember the sweetness of Adrian's constant
cuddling, the warmth of his spirit, the kindness of his hugs,
his devotion to her. Maybe that would be enough to make
her want him back, for her sake more than his.

I could see how wanting Adrian for her own comfort
would be understandable. I remember when my mother
used to wake me up in the middle of the night and rock
me in her rocker when she was scared by the thunder,
during the years after she had left my first father and
before she had met her second husband. I remember
feeling like her companion, that, from when I was very
young, she treated me more like a peer than a child. I could
see why Grace might send for Adrian. In my mind, that
would have been a selfish act, since he would then have

been shuttled back and forth between different schools in very small towns in southern Idaho, between Damion's house, where he abused Grace and the children, and homeless shelters and other temporary places Grace found to get away from his abuse. Despite the reasons that coming for Adrian wouldn't have been good for him, I could see how, in her lowest and loneliest times, Grace might do that.

Grace didn't come for him, though. The whole first year. Lucky for him. Lucky for me. And a testimony to her ability to put stability for Adrian above trying to find her way out of her loneliness through him. By April I had gotten the guardianship papers. Finally, I had the court-approved papers, I had some legal protection against an impulsive act by Adrian's grandmother, or a change of heart by his mother. My lawyer said that Grace would now have to do a number of things if she wanted Adrian to live with her again. First, she would, most likely, have to move to Massachusetts and establish residency. Then, she would need to pay for a lawyer to represent her in court. And she would need to show that there were substantial reasons why Adrian should leave me.

In the wee hours, when I worried about losing Adrian, the lawyer's words comforted me. After I got the papers, I breathed a little deeper. I think Adrian could tell. We both settled down in a way we hadn't before. He seemed to say what was on his mind a little more easily. And he started talking more about the future. "When I am in sixth grade, can I start playing the drums?" "When our oldest dog is very old, will the other doggies give her the dog bed every night?" "When I go to college, I might live away from home. I'm just telling you now so you can get prepared."

It wasn't until I met Grace for the first time, when she took the bus from New York City to Boston this week, that I realized that falling back on "legal protection" wasn't a genuine option. In my mind, my legal rights had been what protected me from losing him. That piece of paper I had xeroxed so Hannah could put it in her safe with her most precious papers had been my protection. With the law on my side, I could argue that he was better off with me—with access to finer schools, a big house in a stable neighborhood, a multiracial community of people who loved him. Until I met Grace, I lay back in the protection of the law—knowing that my whiteness, my class, my professional life, my constant caring for him would all work in my favor. I knew that those were unfair advantages that the courts would use against Grace whether I liked it or not. The papers were my protection. My space of comfort. My way of settling in.

Once I met Grace, all that began to crumble. The minute I saw the way she gently rubbed the back of Adrian's neck and head right after giving him a big hug in the bus terminal, once I saw the way she touched him tenderly in the same exact spots I have touched him this year, the legal defense no longer protected me.

In late July, Grace had called to say that she was moving back to New York. She had left Damion, it seemed for good, and Damion had finally signed papers granting Grace full custody of Adam and Josie. Living in Idaho with two children as a single mother had become absolutely untenable. Grace's mother offered her a basement apartment in her house in New York City. Grace had packed her belongings and shipped eighty-two boxes to New York with the help of someone from her Seventh-Day Adventist church who had access to cheap shipping. When Grace called to tell me of the move, I felt happy for her because it sounded as if the eight years of constant abuse were finally over, and scared by what her being closer to Boston might mean for Adrian and me. After she got settled in her apartment she called to say she wanted to see Adrian. She cited the date—August fourth—as the day over a year ago when she had last seen Adrian.

To celebrate the anniversary of our first year together, Adrian, a friend of mine, and I had done a two-part ritual in a beach town in New York. First we went in search of the biggest sundae we could find. Since we were in New York, not Boston, Adrian and I had to admit that no sundae would be as good as the one we could get at the neighborhood ice-cream store—J. P. Licks. It simply couldn't be. But we were willing to settle for second best, for the sake of the ritual, since we were both sure that no anniversary celebration could be performed without ice cream. Ice cream had been right at the center from the first day Adrian came to visit. Everyone ate ice-cream cake at the ritual welcoming Adrian to the community in the fall. We had eaten ice-cream cones on days when he came home emotionally beat-up from school. On Thanksgiving. At Christmas. On Martin Luther King Day. For Passover. Certainly for his birthday. For the anniversary, we ate huge sundaes. With extra mix-ins. Hot fudge and hot caramel. All over his face. On his shirt. On his hands. Like always.

After that, we headed for the beach where, according to Adrian, we had to do a ritual as close to the water's edge as possible—to honor the passage of time and the ocean as a body of great protection. He collected a bunch of pretty shells, which we put in a circle close to the water's edge. We made a circle with our bodies surrounding the circle of shells and squatted as the waves lapped at our feet. Then we named the best memories of the year — the community ritual welcoming Adrian to Jamaica Plain; Adrian learning how to swim; Adrian having his own room with a computer; his finishing a year at school with glowing reports; rides in the bumper boats on Cape Cod with Hannah and Diana; his love for the dogs; our time eating dinner (often Thai takeout) and watching *Jeopardy* together after I picked him up after my long days of teaching. As the water came closer and closer to our circle of shells, we sped up our celebration, laughing when one big wave completely demolished the moat we had built to prevent the shells from being washed out to sea.

We watched as the tide took the circle of shells away, a washing that Adrian said meant our wishes and happiness would now be safe in the ocean. Then, at my friend's suggestion, we dug a hole meant to hold handfuls of sand that we began to throw in — each handful representing something we were willing to let go of from the year. Adrian loved that part of the ritual, grabbing handfuls of sand and then, with increasing zest on each throw, calling out what he was quite willing to say good-bye to. "Damion!" he shouted. "That Damion be gone forever." He threw a big handful of sand into the pit. Hard and strong. Then another handful with the cry, "People who are mean to children anywhere." More sand. More handfuls. Then, "Injustice against children." And then in the affirmative Adrian shouted, "Children's right to justice." By then, all three of us were throwing sand into the hole — one handful after another, fast and furiously. Falling on ourselves. Falling on the sand. Getting lapped up by the waves. Laughing at each other. Watching the waves take what we threw into the pit out to sea. Finally, as we were holding each other, laughing, Adrian looked up, water at his ankles, sand all over his body, smiled into the sun, and concluded, "Good ritual, huh? Especially the ice cream." A spontaneous ritual at the end of what had turned out to be, usually out of necessity, a spontaneous year. Shells out to the sea. Hole filled with water. Sun streaming down on all of us.

My guess is that Grace's August fourth anniversary of her last seeing Adrian was much different from Adrian's and mine. She probably was en route to New York City around that time, on a bus with her two younger kids, with her boxes of things to follow. Moving again. The umpteenth time. This time to higher ground although, as it turns out, only temporarily, since Grace reunited with Damion again a short while after moving back to New York. Given the profundity of anniversaries, the way they work on you whether you remember them consciously or not, I wasn't surprised when Grace called soon after the fourth to say that she wanted to visit — to see Adrian, who, she said, would no doubt be taller than she could imagine.

The day she was to arrive, Adrian and I got to the bus terminal early. I was afraid that traffic might make us late so I allowed extra time. Adrian wanted to be there even earlier, perhaps a year earlier at least. As we waited, Adrian worried that she might not recognize him. I told him that I could guarantee she would know him. Silently, I remembered Toni Morrison's line in *Beloved* about how a mother can always tell who her child is, even by just seeing the shape of the hand, the contours of the bone under young skin. As it turns out, I was so busy looking at Adrian's face, so busy assuring him that the recognition would be instantaneous, that we didn't see Grace coming until we had run smack into her as we walked down the center of the terminal.

During their initial greeting—with the tenderness of her touch on his neck, the incredible familiarity in the way he tucked under her arm—I first felt the little piece of earth that had begun to feel steady under my feet start to shake. By the end of the visit, late that evening when we drove her back to the terminal and waved good-bye to her until the bus pulled out of sight, I felt there was nothing left of that steady earth. The earth had become sand and the sand had been washed right out from under my feet. I still understood that I had some legal protection. A piece of paper in my file cabinet and in Hannah's safety deposit box gave me the right to power of attorney, the right to enroll him in school, the right to make decisions on his behalf. But this woman, his mother, loved him. I could legally try to stop her if she wanted him back. But ethics were another story.

Somehow, I had not expected Grace to be so steady with him, so confident. She had sounded so broken, so shaky, so little in many of our phone conversations, as Damion continued to try to humiliate her and as she continued to have trouble leaving him. I had not fully expected that the same woman who had been beaten for so long, who had left Andrea in key ways years ago, who had sometimes not called for weeks at a time last fall, would pick up exactly where she had left off with Adrian once she saw him again.

During our several hours together, Grace was the ultimate in graciousness to me, letting me know that she supported my mothering in big and little ways. She asked me many times during the day if Adrian had listened to me during the year. She asked me if he had helped me out enough. She noticed when Adrian didn't know where to put away one of the dinner plates. "What's that about, Adrian? You should know exactly where that goes. You should be doing the dishes all of the time." "Put that stuffed animal back right, like she had it," she admonished him, pointing to me. "On top of Madeline. Keep your things nice, Adrian. Help her out." She chided Adrian when he didn't comb his hair carefully enough. She got on him when he didn't refill the ice tray.

In the hours we had together, we circled back many times to conversations about parenting: that we both couldn't believe how wild some children are allowed to be; that reading everyday was essential — no ifs, ands, or buts; that 10 percent of an accomplishment was talent, the other 90 percent was hard work; that no amount of poverty or racism would stop her from making her home pretty, planting flowers, using baskets (twenty-five cents a piece at secondhand stores) to store things when she couldn't afford furniture.

The day of her visit, Grace brought two mangoes and codfish and dumplings, which she had wrapped in a plastic container and carried all the way on the bus from New York to Boston. I bought swordfish and chicken. Swordfish, if that sounded good to her and she didn't want to cook. Chicken, if she was willing to make her chicken curry, which, I told her, I had been hearing about forever. She opted for the chicken. I followed her around, writing down the amounts for garlic, onions, pepper, chilies, and curry as she cooked. Both of us staying on Adrian, teaching him how to use the garlic press right and then clean it with a toothpick. Both of us letting him know that boys and girls both learn how to cook. That he was going to need to learn how to make curry for others and rice so fluffy that it raised the top of the pan up in its final minutes of cooking.

The day of the visit, Grace came steady. She came loving Adrian—as she had when he was with her, in the last year, and continuing. She came willing to back me up— to remind Adrian that I was in charge. That the best thing he could do for his baby brother and sister was to be his best self—especially in school. The only place we seemed to part that day, when it came to beliefs about mothering, was when Adrian started to cry about missing his three-year-old brother, Adam. Big tears falling on his curry, only half-eaten on his plate—the food too much for him on this biggest of big days. I reached over to him, about to say, "It's okay, Adrian. You can cry. It's hard not seeing Adam. You didn't abandon him, though. It is not your fault." All words I had said to him before. But before the words came out, Grace said, "Stop crying, Adrian. If you cry, I can't bring Adam to you. You need to be a big boy." Gender socialization teaching boys to stuff tender emotions from my perspective, but from hers, who knows? Adrian's tears seemed to be too much for her. Understandably.

I don't know if I could have done what Grace did that day. She came. She was steady. I could feel her deep love for Adrian. See it. Almost touch it. He could, too, and did, clearly. After dinner, she explained how her mother has accused her of not loving Adrian, accused her of being a bad mother. She looked at me. Looked at him. Told us both, eyes between us, that it was love that helped her send him to me. "It would have been selfish to keep you,

Adrian," she told him. "You would have been shuffled back and forth, back and forth, yet another year. You wouldn't have known where your dinner was coming from. You need stability, Adrian. I love you, Adrian, always."

We take her back to the bus terminal—an 8 P.M. bus so that she'll get back by 1 A.M., before the morning, when the woman from her new church who is looking after the younger children will need to go home to get ready to begin her workday. Adrian holds his mother tight as she stands in a long line in the terminal, in front of the door to the bus. A slow-moving line that barely inches forward. She hugs him one more time and then points to me, standing a few feet away. She shows that he needs to go stand with me now. She sends him in my direction before she is through the line, although she could have still held him a few minutes longer. Maybe she wants to avoid the possible drama if they separate at the last possible second. Maybe she needs her body to herself, to prepare for the separation while still being able to keep him in her sight.

He comes to me and I turn him toward her, wrap my arms around him from behind. He whispers in a small voice that he needs to go with her—that he needs to see Josie and Adam. But there is no clarity in his voice. No demand. It is as if he wanted to say it while hearing me say "No," while he could feel my body hold him tight. I hold him, saying, "Your place is here with me, Adrian." His body relaxes in my arms. Then he starts to cry those big, big tears of his. His mother looks back through the weaving line of people. Sees him cry. Looks away. I whisper, "There will be time to cry, Adrian. But not now. Your mom doesn't want to see you cry." He wipes his tears on his shirt. I give him a look of pretend consternation. He knows,

I know, that there is to be no wiping his nose on his shirt. That is what tissues are for. He smiles a little smile, knowing that for this one instance, I won't make him go get a tissue.

His mother gets on the bus. Adrian walks away slowly, hands in his pockets. From behind, he has a stoop that makes him look like a ten-year-old old man. I wait to be sure she gets a seat, hopefully close to the front of the bus. The bus pulls out. I turn around. Adrian is nowhere in sight. I walk toward the elevator and catch him sneaking around pillars and corners, wanting me to chase him, wanting me to run around the terminal to try to catch his quick body. I try unsuccessfully for a couple of rounds. Then I head toward the elevator. Adrian is out of sight. The elevator opens. I get in. At the last possible second, Adrian jumps in the elevator beside me. Laughing at me. That he outran me, again.

We go home to the dogs and enough chicken curry for at least three nights of hot dinners to come. And two huge mangoes, just waiting to be peeled and sucked. We decide to save them until tomorrow, since it is so late and Adrian has track and field camp early the next morning. He starts to get cranky. Tries to pick a fight with me. I fall for it for a moment, but then catch him in the act. I send him to his room for five minutes to sit in his rocker and think. He does it. He apologizes for trying to fight with me. I kiss his face. Multiple kisses. Again and again.

I ask him, "Adrian, remember before your mom came, you told me that you would be all right when she left because once you saw her, you would be able to picture her in your heart again. Is that still true?" He says, "Not really. I miss her and the kids. It's hard." We get him ready for bed. He tells me I better not eat the mangoes while he is asleep. Lights out. I lay beside him quietly for a few minutes. Our nighttime ritual together. The glow-in-the-dark planets on his ceiling begin to light up. His breathing starts to slow down.

Eventually, he falls asleep after showing up at the living-room door a few times with reasons why he can't go to bed. "I can't fall asleep. Crabs might try to bite me." "Make crab cakes, Adrian, for my dinner. Go back to bed," I tell him. Ten minutes later. "Can one of the dogs sleep with me?" "Take Sonic," I relent. "She'll let you drag her up even though she is already asleep." Five minutes later. "You forgot to give me dessert." Typical ten-year-old.

Finally he's asleep. I sit up on the couch, way into the night, mostly staring. Cherríe Moraga, in *Waiting in the Wings: Portrait of a Queer Motherhood* (about the first year of mothering a child who almost died multiple times), quotes from the I Ching. "This time is a subtle study in non-action as a way of attaining real meaning in your life."[1] This time for me, with Adrian, is a study in non-action. It means knowing that, ultimately, I am not in charge. The law will not decide where Adrian will be. Love is bigger than the law. I want to hold Adrian tight. Tight. Tight. I am not alone in this wanting. We both—his mother and I—know how to do it.

Acknowledgments

A BOUT THE NAMING OF NAMES. This little book birthed itself in essays chronologically, one every two weeks or so over the course of Adrian's and my first year together. During these sessions, the essay would write itself all at once, often with no notice at all, whether I was close to my desk, or driving my car, or on my way to deliver a talk on a completely different topic. After the essay would come out, I would feel completely spent, sometimes amazed by its arrival, sometimes overcome with grief, always sure that no such experience would happen again. After eight of these birthing sessions, I began to see that "something was forming," although I spoke very cautiously and only to a couple of people about the process, for fear that naming it might make it disappear. Given that most of the writing I have done previously could accurately be described as getting blood from a stone, the most honest way to talk about the writing of this book is that I felt visited, guided, accompanied as each essay emerged. I say this in relation to "the naming of names" because I don't feel like I wrote this book on my own. The book came through me with a spirit I feel incredibly grateful to have experienced.

More about names. Initially, I decided to use a pen name when this book was published and to change all the names in the text. As a friend of mine said at the time when I made that decision, "Neither Adrian nor Andrea needs to be poster children for anyone." This same friend also told me about Christopher Robin, of *Winnie the Pooh* fame, who, it turns out, never forgave his father for using his name in writing his children's story. Worries that Adrian might feel like Christopher Robin haunted me. Although I felt sad that a pen name would mean I could not speak openly about the book, my desire to protect Adrian's privacy reigned. Or so I thought.

Weeks before the book went into production, a woman who has known me for a long time took a decidedly different approach to the issue of naming. From her perspective, far more damaging than the possible ambivalence that Adrian might feel about having a piece of his story made public would be the message that, as his mother, I was willing to abandon myself by using a pen name. Her position, as a mother of two now-grown children, was never abandon yourself for your children. Never. From my friend's view, to use a pen name was, in fact, leaving myself behind, since writing is so much a part of who I am. Her other question to me — why would you want to be anonymous when anonymity is what you have struggled against all your life?

There is no right answer to this dilemma as far as I can tell, a conundrum that Adrian somehow took in his own hands when he announced one day that he wanted to read the book, "start to finish." So he did, in three sittings, during which time he laughed, got sad, and along the way took out a few passages that he found "too personal" or "embarrassing." We talked a lot as he read, about what he remembered and what he was feeling. As he read, he wanted us to sit side by side, practically on top of each other. Lots of hugging. Lots of closeness. I learned more about him. He was right out there about the passages he wanted me to take out. In our times together, he referred to me three times as his mother (which he had never before done in my presence). "I have two moms," he told me. "You and her. She and you." A claiming session that brought us toward each other. Happily so.

As he read I realized I had been underestimating him. I had no idea he could read fifty pages at a time and speak so clearly about the few passages we needed to leave out. He seemed fine about my using my own name, as long as we still changed all the names in the text. With his pseudonym, he could choose which people to tell — and not — about who he was in the book. He chose his own pseudonym — a name that started with the same initial as his sister's chosen name. He most liked the part of the book where I admit that he outran me in a football game. The naming of names. Its own complication. The final question asked by my friend who advised me to use my own name: what will it say to Adrian if you write about your love for him and then distance yourself from that love with a pseudonym? Her question and Adrian's response to the manuscript were my turning points. My name goes on the book, complicated as that may be.

More about my appreciations and gifts given. Thank you to Doug Armato for flying across country to eat Cuban food with me and believing in my work. Working with the talented people at the University of Minnesota Press, including Gretchen Asmussen, Kathryn Grimes, Amy

Acknowledgments

Unger, Laura Westlund, Linda Lincoln, Adam Grafa, and Patricia Haswell, continues to be a pleasure. A special thank you to Jeanne Lee for her spectacular cover design. Thank you to Jane Lazarre and Maureen Reddy for your compassionate reviews. Thank you to Sarah Stearns for bringing us joy and the ocean. Thank you to David Wellman, Roland Merullo, Amanda Stearns, Lisa Hall, Elly Bulkin, Sohaila Abdulali, Afaa Michael Weaver, Carolyn Villers, Tope Oluwole, Ruth Frankenberg, Lata Mani, Diane Ducharme, Bonnie Kerness, and David Gilbert for your presence in my life and your kind and generous reading. Thank you to Susan Kosoff for being home base, time and time again. For listening to every word and worry. For your magnetic conscience. To Sheila Hart, for pointing me toward an emotional center. To Katie Cannon for your just presence in the world and saying yes, Becky, you can use your own voice. And to Andrea and Adrian, at the center of my heart.

Notes

What part of the story do I tell?

1. Cherríe Moraga and Gloria Anzaldúa, eds., *This Bridge Called My Back: Writings by Radical Women of Color* (New York: Kitchen Table Women of Color Press, 1983).

2. Mari Matsuda, *Where Is Your Body? And Other Essays on Race and Gender and the Law* (Boston: Beacon Press, 1996).

3. Marilyn Buck, David Gilbert, and Laura Whitehorn, *Enemies of the State: A Frank Discussion of Past Political Movements, Victories and Errors, and the Current Political Climate for Revolutionary Struggle within the U.S.A.* A Resistance in Brooklyn Publication. Matt Meyer c/o WRL, 339 Lafayette Street, New York, N.Y. 10012.

In the age of no innocence

1. Mab Segrest, *My Mama's Dead Squirrel: Lesbian Essays on Southern Culture* (Ithaca, N.Y.: Firebrand, 1985).

2. Marita Golden, *Saving Our Sons: Raising Black Children in a Turbulent World* (New York: Doubleday, 1995).

3. Ibid., 11.

4. Jane Lazarre, *The Mother Knot* (Durham, N.C.: Duke University Press, 1976); Jane Lazarre, *Beyond the Whiteness of Whiteness: Memoir of a White Mother of Black Sons* (Durham, N.C.: Duke University Press, 1996); Maureen T. Reddy, *Crossing the Color Line: Race, Parenting and Culture* (Brunswick, N.J.: Rutgers University Press, 1994); Maureen T. Reddy, ed., *Everyday Acts against Racism* (Seattle: Seal, 1996).

In the gaze, in the tone of the voice

1. Andrea O'Reilly, "Ain't That Love? Antiracism and Racial Constructions of Motherhood," in Maureen T. Reddy, ed., *Everyday Acts against Racism* (Seattle: Seal, 1996), 90.

2. Ibid.

Notes

Much of the script, already written

1. Angela Davis, "Afro Images: Politics, Fashion and Nostalgia," in *Names We Call Home: Autobiography on Racial Identity,* ed. Becky Thompson and Sangeeta Tyagi (New York: Routledge, 1996), 87.

2. George Breitman, ed., *Malcolm X Speaks: Selected Speeches and Statements* (New York: Grove Weidenfeld, 1965), 49.

Mother love

1. Andrea O'Reilly, "Ain't That Love?"

2. Ibid., 96–97.

3. Shelley Park, "Mothering across Racial and Cultural Boundaries," in *Everyday Acts against Racism,* 228.

Sex education in the 1990s

1. James Baldwin, *The Fire Next Time* (New York: Dial Press, 1963), 57.

Sand beneath my feet, the tide takes its turn

1. Cherríe Moraga, *Waiting in the Wings: Portrait of a Queer Motherhood* (San Francisco: Firebrand Press, 1997), 61.

Becky Thompson is associate professor of sociology at Simmons College. She is the author of *A Hunger So Wide and So Deep: A Multiracial View of Women's Eating Problems* (Minnesota, 1994) and the coeditor (with Sangeeta Tyagi) of *Names We Call Home: Autobiography on Racial Identity* and *Beyond a Dream Deferred: Multicultural Education and the Politics of Excellence* (Minnesota, 1993). Her book *A Promise and a Way of Life: White Antiracist Activism* is forthcoming from the University of Minnesota Press.